Casa Angelica

Casa Angelica

Arlene's Legacy

Rena Arrigoni

UNIVERSITY OF NEW MEXICO PRESS   *Albuquerque*

"Can't Smile Without You" recorded by Barry Manilow;
By Chris Arnold, David Martin, and Geoff Morrow
© 1975 Dick James Music Limited. All rights for the United States and Canada
controlled by Dick James Music, Inc.
International copyright secured. All rights reserved. Used by permission.

The names of all children at Casa Angelica and the names of my first two
physicians have been changed.

*All author proceeds earned from sales and royalties are being donated to Casa
Angelica Foundation.*

Library of Congress Cataloging-in-Publication Data

Arrigoni, Rena, 1926–
Casa Angelica : Arlene's legacy / Rena Arrigoni.—1st ed.
p.   cm.
ISBN 0-8263-1808-8. —ISBN 0-8263-1809-6 (pbk.)
1. Arrigoni, Arlene, 1956–1978.   2. Handicapped children—New
Mexico—Biography.   3. Handicapped children—Institutional care—New
Mexico.   4. Parents of handicapped children—New Mexico.   5. Casa
Angelica (Foundation)—History.   I. Title.
HV889.N6A77   1997
362.4'0485'0978961–dc21   97-4744
                                                                                      CIP

This book is dedicated to
Arlene's loving father, and my husband, Al;
her two sisters, Regina and Annette;
and to William K. Woodard, M.D.,
the physician at Casa Angelica,
who felt this story needed to be told.

Contents

Illustrations following pages   55 and 113

Foreword

 This book will touch your heart!

It is a true story about people who respect the dignity of human life and have founded and maintained a home for children born with severe disabilities. *Casa Angelica: Arlene's Legacy* is a book about the tireless efforts of the parents of a seriously handicapped child, Arlene, who needed around-the-clock care that could not be provided at home. Realizing there were other children with similar disabilities Al and Rena Arrigoni, Arlene's parents, recruited help from the community and the skills and dedication of the Rome-based Canossian Daughters of Charity, who came to Albuquerque to open Casa Angelica in 1967.

The facility goes far beyond just keeping the children clean, safe, and dry. The book shows the progress made in providing love and caring that includes developing the potential of each child to learn and to grow, and to reach the highest level of independence and self-reliance possible. Therapy and individual attention enable children to reach physical, mental, emotional, and spiritual development.

As Archbishop of Santa Fe and a friend of Casa Angelica, I salute this book as a real inspiration to those seeking to bring joy and loving care to others.

Most Rev. Michael J. Sheehan, S.T.L., J.C.D.
Archbishop of Santa Fe

Preface

 This book is the story of Casa Angelica, which opened its doors in 1967 as New Mexico's first privately operated nursing home for youngsters with severe disabilities. But to tell the story of this residence and the Canossian Daughters of Charity who direct it, I have to bring you into our family from 1956 to 1978 and especially into the life of our daughter, Arlene.

My hope is that by sharing our experiences I can provide some support and comfort to families parenting children with disabilities. For many years we worked to overcome numerous obstacles in our effort to create a facility that stressed love and an active life for Arlene consistent with a high level of care and medical attention. To do so required constant advocacy—to always push for the rights of children with special needs in a world that still does not readily accept them.

When people of goodwill do come together to help children with disabilities, truly wonderful things happen. That is the message of Casa Angelica and a part of Arlene's legacy. I hope that everyone reading this book will see in Arlene's life, and in Casa Angelica, a reminder of the power of hope and an example of the good that is possible when people reach out to help others.

Acknowledgments

I want to especially thank my friend Carol Cohea for helping me put my thoughts and words into a narrative for this book. She is a native of Albuquerque and a graduate of the University of New Mexico, where she earned a degree in journalism. She has worked as a newspaper reporter and trade magazine editor and is currently a public relations consultant.

My family and I cannot in the space allotted here begin to mention, much less to thank once again, the hundreds and hundreds of New Mexicans—individuals, families, and businesses—who gave and still give time, support, funds, furnishings, construction labor and maintenance skills, and who continue to visit the nuns and children and help in so many ways. The Arrigonis and the Casa Angelica family know who you are and keep you in their prayers. You are forever part of the amazing story of Casa Angelica.

We would like to acknowledge all Casa Angelica Foundation past and present board members.

FOUNDATION PAST AND PRESENT BOARD MEMBERS

Albert Arrigoni
Regina Arrigoni,
Rena Arrigoni
Charles Campbell
John Craig

Mrs. Mary Craig
John Dwyer
Mrs. Agnes Fanning
Reginald Garcia
Philip Hubbell

Mrs. Jo Eckert Huber
Ed Jory
Mrs. Jan Keleher
William Keleher
Don Kirby
A.W. La Pine
Mrs. Marge Legette
Joseph Lopez
Peter McCanna
Mrs. Myra McKay

Mrs. Anna McCulloch
Mrs. Inez Phillips
Mrs. Elizabeth Quinn
Benjamin Raskob
Will Raskob
Gen. Emmanuel Schifani
Mrs. Julia Seligman
Mrs. Johnnie Sue Stiff
Mrs. Ella Watson
Dr. William Kay Woodard

We would also like to thank the Casa Angelica Auxiliary Past and Present Presidents:

AUXILIARY PAST AND PRESENT PRESIDENTS

Mrs. Anna McCulloch
1967-69
Mrs. Genevieve Rossi
1969–70
Mrs. Lyn Kil
1970–71
Mrs. Adele Davis
1971–72
Mrs. Edith Todesco
1972–73
Mrs. Peggy Brennan
1973–74
Mrs. Marge Doherty
1974–75
Mrs. Rosemary Vaio
1975–76
Mrs. Jane McKenna
1976–77
Mrs. Janet Lederle
1977–78

Mrs. Jan Keleher
1978–79
Mrs. Jo Koller
1979–80
Mrs. Carole Christensen
1980–81
Mrs. Jotina Trussell
1981–82
Mrs. Rosemary Vaio
1981–82
Mrs. Betty Cummings
1983–84
Mrs. Becky Vokes
1984–85
Mrs. Mary Ellen Rock
1985–86
Mrs. Jotina Trussell
1986–87
Mrs. Sandra Tybor
1987–88

Mrs. Nancy Ingram
1988–89
Mrs. Kathryn Godfrey
1989–90
Mrs. Leonor A. Mead
1990–91
Ms. Lindsey Hovden
1991–92
Mrs. Elizabeth Thompson
1992–93

Mrs. Shanaz Arman
1993–94
Mrs. Mandy Arrington
1994–95
Mrs. Dorothy Fritz-Gerald
1995–96
Mrs. Nikki MacDonald
1996–97

I also want to acknowledge the editorial suggestions of Elizabeth J. Roll, Ph.D.

CHAPTER ONE

The Birth of an Angel

THE CLEAR, crisp chimes of the chapel bell float on the New Mexico air. They carry on the breeze across the South Valley alfalfa fields and apple orchards, green and fragrant with the warm smell of summer. Three times a day—at six in the morning, noon, and six in the evening—the bell chimes the Angelus and marks time. During those sunny hours, when song sparrows chirp in the tall, stately cottonwoods and roosters crow from barnyard to barnyard, one hears the neighborhood children laugh and call to each other. Their shrieks of laughter seem to blend with the peals of the bell of Casa Angelica, taking me back to another time and place, and the memory of a child.

Arlene Ida Arrigoni—Arlene, Arlenie, Arlie. She was born October 10, 1956, in the dark of night. I despise the night; night cast a shadow on the birth of this, my second child, a beautiful, dark-eyed girl with brown, curly hair.

The baby was four days overdue and in breech position. Doctors in the delivery room at Albuquerque's St. Joseph's Hospital induced labor. I sensed things weren't going right. There was a curious quiet in the delivery room. This delivery seemed so complicated and different from Regina's birth just a year and four days before in the same hospital. This was an era with no labor-coaches, or fathers in the delivery room. I lay wide awake with only a saddleblock to numb the pains of an exhausting twenty-four-hour labor. Instead of joy and expectation, gloom and sadness prevailed. No lusty cry announced Arlene's arrival. Behind white surgical masks, doctors talked briefly and in muffled tones about the umbilical cord. In the mirror overhead, I caught a glimpse of a short blue-veined cord.

Finally, my baby was brought to me, all five pounds two ounces of angel. She looked so tiny in the doctor's large white-gloved hands. There was no chance to touch or hold her, no chance for immediate maternal bonding. The doctor presented her to me much as a waiter holds a bottle of wine for the diner's inspection and approval. Despite her bluish-white pallor and her silent, no-tears arrival, she seemed a perfect doll. Then I looked into her eyes. Something was wrong with her eyes! My heart quickened and my exhaustion was gone, replaced by near panic. Was it my imagination? Her beautiful brown eyes seemed veiled, as if she were looking at me through a gossamer film.

"Doctor," I cried out, "what's wrong with my baby? There's something wrong with my little girl! Her eyes are so gray, so veiled, so sad."

That was the beginning. First came the appeasing, "Rena, you're just a worrier, an emotional Italian mother. There's nothing wrong with Arlene."

Then came the problems. She was put into an isolette where she began her struggle to survive. She couldn't suckle right. She became jaundiced. There were continual bouts of vomiting, convulsions, and lethargy. She got diarrhea. She became dehydrated. And finally, on the third day, she contracted pneumonia.

I stood beside the isolette that day and shook my head in disbelief. Intravenous needles were taped to her tiny head. It was the only place the doctors and nurses could find veins easily. As healthy babies were being discharged from the hospital, I had to stand and watch my child struggling to breathe. Anguish and fear for my baby tore at me. What happened? What went wrong? What's happening to her? Why won't they tell me? The doctors must know, surely they know.

My husband said he remembered this as "the saddest day of my life." Looking back now, Al realizes how young he was and how he couldn't believe it was happening.

"I know my family history," he said. "Our family has lived for three to four hundred years in the same village in Italy. Nothing like this has ever happened."

It was the same in my family—a long history in the same village and no birth defects or mental retardation. Where had this come from? Al went to the hospital every day and spent so much time there that the receptionist, Bertha Ruvolo, became his close friend. He tells me now that when he looked at Arlene from the window of the isolette, he would try to figure out what life would be like for his new daughter. He tried to picture her childhood and plan ahead for her.

When I visited Arlene, I couldn't touch my tiny baby. I would grip the side of the cold, metal isolette. It was as if a glass coffin encased her, separating her from me. If only I could hold her, then things would become real. This was surely a bad dream. She would awaken like a tiny Sleeping Beauty and again become that seemingly perfect baby I had hoped to give birth to. But no, I could only continue to clutch the isolette as the tears began to well up in my eyes, then run down my cheeks. Finally, there was no holding back the painful sobs. I was only dimly aware of the nurses supporting me and helping me to a wheelchair, then rolling me back to my room. I was told later that I had gone into shock, and that the doctors had ordered me sedated.

As Arlene's condition continued to deteriorate, Al arranged for her to be baptized in the hospital. My sister, Louise, and brother-in-law, Roland, became godparents by proxy.

In spite of the mind-numbing sedatives, I lay in the hospital bed, staring at the white ceiling. I attempted to grapple with my newborn's helplessness, and wondered if this was to be my last sight of her. Once again, I cried as I listened to the happy noises of infants being brought to other mothers. Over and over, I asked myself, "Could this be happening to me?" My tiny baby clung desperately to life, or was she merely shunning death? Such tenacity was a characteristic she would display over and over.

Five days later, without the fog of sedation, I left the hospital empty-handed, confused, somber, depressed and heartbroken. Al drove our '52 Chrysler home that mid-October Monday. Hardly a word was said between us. There were no words left to say. I stared dismally out the car window, wondering how the lives of others could seem to go on normally while mine plunged into pain and uncertainty.

When I arrived home my mother came to greet us and noticed that we were not carrying our new born. Regina toddled to meet us at the door.

"Arlene can't come home yet," I answered and started to cry. Regina studied my face, then looked at Al, whose grim expression was enough to satisfy her one-year-old curiosity. She retreated to another room to play.

I, too, retreated to the kitchen with Mama who had returned to the supper she'd been preparing. We said nothing as I stood silently beside her. Just having her near comforted me, and brought me a measure of security.

Arlene spent a month at St. Joseph's Hospital while doctors tested her, searching for a clue to her illness. The cause was elusive. Why did she continue to lose weight? Why was her breathing so labored? Why the chronic diarrhea? My heart cried out, "What's wrong with my baby?"

Three times a day for the next month, I left Regina at home with my mother and traveled to the hospital to feed Arlene. I sat amid healthy, pink babies, each time an entirely new group, rocking in an old-fashioned, wooden rocking chair, trying to see if I could get my little darling to gain one ounce. Not pounds, just an ounce! While other babies began a chorus of cries for their feedings, Arlene lay motionless in my arms: quiet, uncomplaining, listless, trying to suck down a drop of the lactose-based formula.

Finally, on November 12th, a little over a month after her birth, the doctors released Arlene from the hospital. I wondered if she was really well enough to leave, or if they were just too frustrated to care for her any longer. She weighed less than six pounds.

At home, the weight-gain battle continued and was complicated by the fact that there was always something drastically wrong with Arlene. She was plagued with ear infections, diarrhea, or high fever. Each problem meant that the few ounces she had gained were quickly lost. We constantly battled with her weight, using it as a measure for her well-being. Each illness meant another visit to the emergency room or doctor's office. She was always on the verge of slipping away from us.

If the strain was beginning to tell on Al, he didn't show it. He maintained a calm exterior by settling into a daily routine. He came home from work, and upon coming through the front door headed for Arlene's bedroom. Gently picking her up, he asked how the day had gone. After changing his clothes, he would bring her into the living room and sit with her, rocking her in his big easy-chair as he watched television. After dinner, he helped bathe Regina and Arlene in the kitchen sink. Then it was bedtime for the girls, and a few hours alone for us. It was a relief just to have him around. With the days as exhausting as they were, watching television was our main distraction. Commercial breaks meant time to check on Arlene and make a quick check on Regina.

While the rest of the family slept, I stayed up with Arlene. These were the days before there were heart and breathing monitors that sound an alarm or signal an abnormality. I was the monitor. Sometimes that simply meant standing over her crib and watching the rise and fall of her tiny chest. At other times, it meant rocking her. Eventually we were to wear out three rocking chairs. When the pale light of dawn finally filtered through the curtains, I knew Arlene and I had made it through another night. Daytime meant it was time for our active toddler.

For several months, day after day, Papa brought Mama early in the morning to spend the whole day. He'd come back to have dinner with us, and then take Mama home. There are no words to describe the support my mother and father gave us during those months of adjusting to caring for a sick child. My wonderful mother was my closest friend, baby-sitter, cook, and housekeeper. She attempted to keep everything under control in my out-of-control world.

By the time Arlene was two months old, she had been put through tests for hydrocephalus, phenylketonuria, and cystic fibrosis. I asked myself, "Why is this child suffering? Why must I see her suffer?"

Three, four, five months passed with the same routine at home. Each day was a battle to defy death. I began to wonder how much more my frayed nerves could take. Amazingly, I kept going. I found some inner reserves of strength and energy that I never thought I had, and I fought on. At six months, Arlene weighed only seven pounds at most. The slightest sickness caused her to lose ounces; she had diarrhea at least once a week and almost always a high fever accompanied by an ear infection. Arlene moved little, though the intense pain of those ear infections made her attempt to tug at her ear. The slightest movement of her hand to her ear signaled the onset of yet another ear infection and an appointment with the doctor.

We were at Dr. Smith's office two or three times every week. On perhaps the fiftieth visit, I had to ask, "What is wrong with my baby? Why are her eyes so veiled?"

Putting the stethoscope down on the examination table, he turned to me. His eyes met mine, and he said, "Why don't you ask her?"

His tone was quiet, but the note of frustration and exasperation could not be mistaken. I could understand both, but I had not prepared myself to hear it in his voice. I stood there in silence, his words echoing "... ask her ... ask her. ..."

Ask a six-month-old child? In disbelief, I stared at him, shocked by his lack of sympathy and concern. Where was his professionalism? Weren't we fighting this battle together? Or was I wrong? Was I the only one fighting? Had he given up? Stiffening, I resolved not to cry in front of this man. Man? I had to wonder about that. Was he a man? Or, was he a monster masquerading as a doctor?

Summoning all my courage, I gathered the pink blankets around my beautiful baby. Without a word to him or his nurse, I walked quickly out of the office. Regina, taking a cue from me, said nothing, and followed close behind. Outside in the bright spring sunshine, I headed for my car. Once safely inside, I began crying. I cried all the way home.

In the driveway, composing myself and once again in control, I charted a new course. "All right," I said with determination, "we'll go to another pediatrician." The next day, I made an appointment with Dr. Jones, Dr. Smith's associate. Both had come highly recommended as the two best pediatricians in Albuquerque in the mid-1950s.

Dr. Jones, like Dr. Smith, was in his mid-thirties. He wore glasses and seemed studious. He was the picture of professionalism and concern as Arlene, Regina, and I were shown into the stark, antiseptic, white examination room—standard for the 1950s. Children's murals and pictures of Bambi and Thumper or the Seven Dwarfs were not to be found in doctors' offices then. The examination completed, Dr. Jones put his instruments down, and once again my fears were confirmed by the expression on his face. But this time the answer was more callous.

"This child is not normal. I won't even give her penicillin to save her. She should die," he said.

The words hung heavily in the air. I wasn't prepared for the abrupt brutality of the statement. It was like a knife had been plunged into my heart.

"My God," I thought to myself, "I can't be hearing this. My baby, my beautiful baby girl, *should* die. Not will die, but should die. It wasn't a prognosis. It wasn't a diagnosis. It was a sentence. A death sentence. This man had played judge and jury. I thought I'd come to a doctor?"

This time, as I bundled the pink blanket around Arlene, my hands shook and trembled with anger and outrage. I said nothing, as before, and together with eighteen-month-old Regina, we quickly headed out the office door and into the car. Once again, safely within the confines of my car, I began to cry. I maneuvered the car out of the parking lot and headed home. As I drove and cried, I glanced at the baby lying on the front seat beside me. The baby who "should die." "It's true," I admitted to myself, "she isn't normal."

Having had one healthy baby eighteen months earlier, I knew that by now Arlene should be sitting up, following movement with her eyes, reaching out to grasp things, and babbling to herself. Instead, she lay passively on the front seat, her immobile arms beside her. She stared straight ahead with those big, gray eyes—veiled and sad.

Regina quietly stared out the window at objects we passed. Usually she laughed and chattered, but she intuitively knew this was a time for silence. At a stoplight, I glanced again at Arlene, then studied Regina and fought the impulse to compare them. I had an eighteen-month-old child whom I didn't even know! All my concern, attention, heartache and worries, for too long, had focused on Arlene. All my time and energy were consumed by Arlene. Already Regina, my little queen, was my helper, my pillar, my strength. Who was Regina? Did I know this child? Was she a toddler or a little old woman? What kind of childhood was she having? Was she even having a childhood? We drove home in silence.

When Al came home, I told him of the doctor's pronouncement. His reaction was one of outrage, totally uncharacteristic of this man. Al recalls how he felt then.

"I believe in helping someone as much as possible. I couldn't see letting Arlene suffer and die that way. I was appalled that someone who'd taken the oath to heal the sick could've suggested such a thing."

We decided that together we would see Dr. Jones. For too long Al had been troubled by Arlene's sickness. For too long this lovable, patient man had kept night vigils, rocking and rocking Arlene until she fell asleep, her tiny head on his broad shoulder, her fragile body in his big hands.

"I never told anyone I didn't have any hope for Arlene," Al says now. "I wanted Rena to have her dreams, but I felt that nature would take its course."

The following day, we arrived at Dr. Jones' office. For this particular visit, we had brought neither of the girls; we left them both at home with Mama. As we sat in the waiting room, our mood was one of anger—anger that it had come to this. Needless to say, we were not kept waiting long. We were shown into Dr. Jones' office. He seated himself behind his desk and motioned to two chairs in front.

"We will not keep our baby under your care," Al declared emphatically. "What recommendation can you give us?"

Dr. Jones recommended the Children's Hospital in Denver. Within a week he personally made arrangements for Arlene to be seen by a pediatrician there named Dr. Robert Fisher. Ironically, only a few months before, Dr. Fisher had been practicing in Albuquerque at the Lovelace Medical Foundation. Thanks to Dr. Randy Lovelace, a pioneer in aerospace medicine, the clinic was to become famous for its involvement with space biomedicine.

The afternoon of April 4th, 1957 we packed a suitcase for the hour-long flight to Denver. Mama came to stay with Regina. As I dressed Arlene, quietly, without Al's knowledge, I took a flashlight from beside the bed and prepared to shine it in her eyes. Standing poised with the light above her, I asked myself if I really wanted to know the answer. Holding my breath, I pushed the "on" button.

As the piercing white light shone on Arlene she didn't blink or turn her head. She stared motionless straight ahead. Panic gripped me and my stomach knotted. "My God, is my baby blind? Do I dare tell Al of my suspicions?"

"No," I answered the unspoken question. I must be strong. Quickly turning off the light, I put it aside before Al could see me with it. Summoning all my courage and strength, I continued to dress her.

Once aboard the plane, the three of us were quiet and somber. As we lifted off the ground, the plane headed east toward the blue haze of the Manzano Mountains and then circled north to carry us to Denver. Usually the ascent would find me peering out the plane's window to catch a glimpse of familiar landmarks below. Not this time. We were an emotion-charged, overwrought couple with a very sick infant. As we flew to Denver, Arlene was running a high fever. I spent the flight holding my baby and worrying about her eyes, thinking over and over: she didn't blink, she didn't blink.

At Stapleton Field, we transferred to a taxi that took us directly to a red brick, two-story hospital, located in downtown Denver. We stepped out of the cab and into the cold dusk. The hospital was in the process of remodeling. Any other time the barricades, ladders and zigzag-maze of paths around construction equipment wouldn't have bothered us, but that night it added to our uneasy, apprehensive feelings.

We were directed downstairs to the basement where a team of four doctors, including Dr. Robert Fisher, met us. Dr. Fisher was of medium height and had dark hair and a dark mustache. Compared to the two previous pediatricians, he appeared to be personable and understanding.

As I handed Dr. Fisher the three-inch thick manila medical file from Albuquerque, my words rushed out, "I think our baby is blind."

The doctors glanced at me. Al turned and stared in shocked disbelief, but he said nothing.

We were led down the corridor to a large room. In the center of the room was the examining table. I laid Arlene on it. As the four doctors poked and prodded her, she lay motionless, staring straight ahead. Finally, they instructed us to leave her with them for further tests.

"Leave her?" I thought, "Leave my little angel? Leave her as if she were some broken clock being left at a repair shop? They'll call us when it's ready."

I fought the urge to snatch Arlene up and run with her, out of the room, down the corridor, out of the hospital. Instead, Al and I nodded our approval. We managed to find our way out of the depths of the hospital. Once again, I left a hospital empty-handed. The same desperate feelings rushed back as on that day in October when I left St. Joseph's Hospital without my newborn.

Outside on the dark street in the cold April night, Al and I walked silently to the Mayflower Hotel, a few blocks away. In one hand, he carried the single suitcase we had brought; with the other, he gripped my hand so tightly I knew he was as apprehensive as I. Once again, as on the day of her birth, the lonely darkness covered me like a cold shroud.

It took the doctors four days to run tests. Al and I spent our time either standing by Arlene's crib, holding and feeding her every four hours, or walking around downtown Denver while she slept.

On the fifth day, Dr. Fisher called us into his office. As he moved behind his desk to sit down, we took chairs facing him. Barely breathing, I sat on the edge of my chair, knowing that in the test results lay Arlene's future.

"Mr. and Mrs. Arrigoni," Dr. Fisher began quietly, but firmly, "your baby is not blind. She has deep cataracts, a condition known as galactosemia."

I gasped and clutched Al's hand. My mind was reeling. "Not blind! Not blind," I felt a flood of relief, for surely if she was not blind, there must be a cure. I tried to concentrate on every word that was being spoken.

"What is galactosemia?" I asked.

"Galactosemia," Dr. Fisher began, "has to do with the milk sugars that caused the cataracts. The cataracts are congenital. She was born with them. A child must be taken off milk products immediately after birth in order for the body's chemistry to rectify the situation. This must be done in the first month following birth or retardation sets in. There's nothing that can be done now to repair the damage."

I stared at Dr. Fisher in disbelief, trying to fully comprehend what was and was not being said. I didn't know whether to cry or be grateful.

"My baby isn't blind," I reassured myself, "No, not blind . . . but irreversibly retarded. My child, my beautiful angel . . . retarded? Was her life to continue to be a life of suffering and sickness because of a missed diagnosis? Such a waste of a little life."

Through tears, I managed to gather Arlene up from the hospital bed where she had spent those four grueling days of tests. Hailing a taxi, we headed for the airport and home, 400 miles away.

One fact faced us now—irreversible mental retardation. Arlene's brain was damaged and as parents and as a family we were going to deal with this—for however long Arlene lived. Could we, as a family, hold up and pull together? What were we to do as parents and as individuals? And finally, how were we to care for her? Nothing in either Al's or my background prepared us for the responsibilities. We had our faith and each other—and an uncertain future.

CHAPTER TWO

A Time of Hope

 MY FAMILY, the Menicuccis, have lived in Albuquerque for over sixty years. My father, Amerigo, and mother, Davina Allesandri Menicucci, both came to America from Lucca, a farming community in northern Italy. Our ethics were forged by work, the nearby Immaculate Conception Church, and St. Mary's Catholic School. Our family was never rich, but happy. A tremendous amount of love filled our home.

At eighteen, I graduated from St. Mary's, and for two years I attended the University of New Mexico on "the hill" just a few miles to the east of downtown Albuquerque. Basically carefree, I had no special goals in mind. I had taken a number of business courses and went to work as a secretary at First National Bank. Though many of the young women my age, with whom I worked, had apartments of their own, I continued to live with my parents.

I was twenty-four when I met a handsome young man from Chicago, Al Arrigoni. At six feet he towered over my five-foot four-inch frame. We soon found we had much in common. His mother Ida Ricci Arrigoni, born a few miles east of Lucca, had immigrated to Chicago with her family. Al's father Albert Arrigoni was born in a small farming community of Molin Nuovo in Tuscany. Eight to ten families lived there and each of the families—except Al's—had someone who had immigrated to Albuquerque. Al's father had gone to Chicago and married Ida in 1925.

While visiting Albuquerque in January 1947, Al's parents were so impressed by the mild winter weather and seeing their Italian friends that they decided to move west. Shortly after their arrival here, Al's mother was found to have cancer. She lived in Albuquerque about a year before her death. Eight months later, Al's father also died of cancer. Al, then twenty-three, was left to raise his fifteen-year-old brother, Roland.

Knowing Al for only a short time, I was enormously impressed with his sense of responsibility, kindness, love, and devotion. We were married in the Immaculate Conception Church on May 2, 1951. Roland, then seventeen, was Al's best man and a member of our family. When we returned from our honeymoon, Roland was waiting, smiling on the porch of our rented apartment at 211½ Cornell SE, ready to move in.

Immediately, we were a family. If Al seemed like a father to Roland, I longed to be a mother, but at the same time, I also knew I was the outsider and the newest member of their family. This was made abundantly clear at dinnertime. Al was an avid sports fan. Roland was a football and baseball player at the University of New Mexico, so sports were the topic of conversation. I was determined to take part and forced myself to learn about football, baseball, and the major players each season.

For four years, as Roland continued his studies at the University of New Mexico, I continued to work at the First National Bank as a secretary. Al worked tirelessly at P. F. McCanna Inc., a real estate and insurance firm. Eventually Al and Wilfred Brennan, his long-time coworker and associate, purchased Berger-Briggs Real Estate and Insurance Inc.

With our combined incomes, we could dream of building our own home for the family we wanted. We yearned for children, but it seemed as if pregnancy was impossible for me. I watched silently and enviously as first my sister-in-law, then my sister, became pregnant and had children. Meanwhile, I went through two miscarriages and worried about my inability to have children. Finally, after one particularly long, soul-searching discussion, Al and I decided to begin adoption proceedings.

Within weeks, I found to my surprise that I was pregnant. This time my pregnancy was an uncomplicated and very joyful nine months. On October 6, 1955, at six on a clear, crisp, sunny morning a beautiful baby girl was born to us. The first feature I noticed about my baby was her eyes. She had big, clear, almond-shaped eyes. She was a beautiful, perfect baby with a soft peaches-and-cream complexion. As Al and I stood at the nursery window several hours after her birth, we chose her name, Regina. It means *queen* in Italian and she was our little queen.

We brought her home to our new house, in what was then considered Albuquerque's far Northeast Heights, at 1328 Lafayette NE. Our first home was a modest three-bedroom flat-roofed house. Al and Roland and Roland's university pals helped with the moving the day I delivered Regina. And as he had four years before, Roland greeted us at the door as we carried in our new arrival.

During the first year, I found myself thrilled with the new role of motherhood—a real mother this time, not someone caught playing a role between mother and big sister. We had wanted a baby so desperately, and here she was, the greatest joy of our lives. Every new movement and development was cause for lengthy discussion—for once surpassing sports at the supper table. Her cries or laughter brought all three of us on the run to soothe the tears or share in the fun. Life was joyous and good.

Regina was three months old when I became pregnant again. Often I'd stop in the middle of my housework to watch Regina play. The thought of having another baby as lovely as she filled me with joy and anticipation. I was thrilled. I had no physical problems. I experienced a little back pain, but perhaps that came from lifting Regina, a healthy infant developing at a normal rate. She was walking and saying a few words by nine months, and we thought she was the smartest little girl in the world, a real gem, so independent, intelligent, sweet and perceptive to moods. All these characteristics would serve her well in the years to come. My whole life revolved around our baby, Regina.

Then came that night in October, a year and four days after Regina's birth. The beauty of that first year was completely overshadowed by the heartache that followed. During the next year, I often wondered if life had ever been so simple, if there had really been a time when life was rosy and good. I was not the type of person who could stand to see even a small creature suffer, and now suddenly my whole world had changed.

CHAPTER THREE

An Angel Never Cries

CARING for a medically fragile child is so over-whelming and all-consuming one can only hope that life goes reasonably well for others in the family. Arlene was always sick, and every day it took all our strength to keep her alive. Then, un-like now, there were no support groups to ease the burden for parents of children with special needs. I felt alone and isolated. I cried. I was depressed.

More than anything, I was frightened that a life-threatening situation would arise while Al was at work and I was alone with the girls. I worried that in one dreadful moment of indecision or hesitation, I would panic and lose Arlene. I had to be ready to respond instantly to any situation and to respond with a cool and level head.

Of that time Al says, "I always had Arlene in the back of my mind. Always. I rocked and bathed her every night. I remember thinking that she was suffering so much that maybe it would be better in some ways if she slipped away. I called home frequently during those days."

Our lives had changed dramatically and drastically. The simple ac-tions and day-to-day routines I took for granted a year earlier with Regina now had no meaning. Feeding Arlene was virtually an endless process. It took an hour-and-a-half just to get an ounce of pureed food in her. But I was fortunate Arlene could be fed with a spoon. So many children in her condition must be tube fed.

There was the constant fear she would choke after she burped up food; unable to turn her head, she could have suffocated. There were the endless periods of rocking and rocking to comfort her and to comfort me because each time I put her down, there was the underlying fear that she would die in her sleep. When I finally surrendered her to the crib, there were the countless crib checks, repeated turning of her body and head from side to side and making sure she was still covered—and alive. Arlene's circulation was so poor her feet were always nearly deep purple-black from the cold. At night she was first dressed in a blanket sleeper, then a winter snow-play bunting.

I learned to think and react for her. Even after three years when we moved her out of our bedroom to her own lovely little peach and white room a few feet down the hall, I found I had become so attuned to her every move that I could hear or sense when she stirred. Parents usually rely on a normal child's cries to alert them to a problem, but I couldn't depend on Arlene to cry. She never cried; she was *never* to cry.

That didn't mean her life was painless. Most likely she was never for a moment without pain. Her knee joints were swollen with arthritis, leaving her incapable of even the slightest pain-free movement. Walking was impossible. Breathing was so visibly painful that it hurt me to watch her. Each breath was a struggle, an audible gasp, so that the hollow of her throat seemed almost to sink to the top of her spine when she inhaled.

For the next few years, the day for the Arrigoni family began at four in the morning. Instantly, I was at her side. After a check to satisfy myself that her breathing was regular—or regular for Arlene—I went into the dark, cold kitchen to warm a bottle, then went back to the bedroom and the rocker to begin feeding. An hour-and-a-half later I would reluctantly put Arlene in her crib. By six Regina was up and padding around the house in her slippers and pajamas. A few minutes later, Al awakened. I was not willing to relinquish this small amount of time alone with the two of them. I eagerly made breakfast for the three of us. Then Al was off to work and I was left with the children.

By eight it was again time to feed Arlene, which would take another hour to an hour-and-a-half. Ten o'clock was snack time for Regina; after a quick lunch for Regina and me, it was back to Arlene for another hour or so. At this point, Regina was usually napping; if all appeared well, I napped, too. To go to sleep as most people use the term was an unheard-of luxury. My sleep was a series of naps, nothing more. Always I was straining to hear Arlene's movements. God forbid that I should be asleep and Arlene would stop breathing. At four I fed Arlene again, then afterward I rushed to fix dinner for Al, Regina, and me. So it went until Arlene's feeding at eight in the evening and then another feeding at midnight—then it would start all over again at four the next morning.

Although this routine became my way of life for years, my body never physically adapted to the schedule. I was in a permanent state of mental and physical exhaustion. I found it difficult to perform even simple tasks, which led me back to my original fear that I wouldn't be able to respond in an emergency. By age two, Arlene, though still severely underweight, was beginning to be a physical challenge to move from crib to chair.

It became a vicious psychological circle. Only if I concentrated on Arlene and focused totally on her needs, could I put aside my fears. As a result, I was Arlene's twenty-four-hour-a-day, seven-day-a-week mother and nurse. After the first six months I could have qualified as a licensed practical nurse.

Arlene's simplest physical functions were a problem. Bowel movements were almost nonexistent. Suppositories and enemas were routine. Impacted bowels were commonplace, and I learned to handle that messy chore.

But some things one never gets used to. For me those were her convulsions. Initially, I didn't know how to handle convulsions. The first occurred when Arlene was a year old. But the scene would be repeated time and time again. Checking on her in bed, I found her turning blue, shaking and convulsing. With only a moment's hesitation, I scooped her into my arms, blanket and all, shouted to two-year-old Regina to get her jacket and follow me. Flying out of the house, I slammed the door behind us and ran to the nearest neighbor at home. We only had one car at that time, so we had to depend on loving and understanding neighbors for frantic hospital runs. We lived only fifteen minutes away from St. Joseph's Hospital, but the trip always seemed slow and arduous.

We went straight to the hospital emergency room. On the table, doctors injected Arlene with medication that not only calmed her convulsions, but put her into a deep and quiet sleep. The sleep was so deep, my new fear was that she would not wake up. Each time, I'd sigh and prepare myself. This is it. My little one won't make it this time. Crises like this left me shaken and completely devastated.

While I was dealing with the day-to-day, moment-to-moment demands, Al was worried about the family's future. Al recalled, "We always had to have full-time help. We were just a young couple starting out, and that was a financial burden. I was struggling. I was helping the company's clients invest in real estate; Albuquerque was growing then, and I could have used some money to invest myself, for our future. But I wasn't able to take advantage of all the opportunities," Al recalls. "We deprived ourselves of a new car, a bigger home, vacations—but our first responsibility was caring for Arlene."

Arlene brought other changes to our lives. Grocery shopping was done by telephone to a store that would deliver. Sunday Mass was accomplished in two shifts. I went alone to early Mass at Our Lady of Fatima Church, while Al stayed home with the babies. This was my quiet time, the time I jealously guarded for myself. The quiet of the church at that early hour refreshed and soothed me. This was a quiet eye in the middle of a dark storm. After church I was able to go home and continue another day.

That was our Sunday routine, except for one Sunday a year. That was Easter. Each Easter morning, I finished Arlene's eight o'clock morning feeding and dressed Regina in her latest Easter outfit, complete with white patent leather shoes, matching purse and white straw hat. I made a pot of coffee and laid out some bakery-fresh cinnamon rolls on a china plate. Promptly at nine, Yale Weinstein, who lived a few houses away, knocked at our door. The Sunday Denver Post was tucked under his arm. A quiet and gracious man of medium build and stature, he imparted confidence and calm. I trusted him implicitly. While I gave him a last-minute rundown of Arlene's current condition and schedule, he'd urge us to get moving or we'd all be late for church.

"Not to worry, not to worry," he reassured me as we hurried out the front door.

Sitting in the pew with Al and Regina beside me almost made me uneasy, and yet I marveled that to most people this was a normal, weekly family event. To us it was an occasion—the only time in the year when we could attend church as a family. I thanked God for Yale Weinstein. After Mass we'd drive downtown to the Alvarado Hotel at the train station for breakfast. Then it was back to the house and Arlene.

Other holidays were far from what the word implied. They were cheerless and agonizing. Christmas, with its cheerful carols, was always incredibly sad. The bright blinking lights mocked our feelings. A life-threatening emergency always seemed to land Arlene in the hospital at Thanksgiving and again at Christmas and New Year's, leaving us with precious little to be thankful for or to sing about. There was no "joy to the world" for us to take the time to share in.

Arlene's illness affected us in other ways. A family run to a drive-in for hamburgers was virtually impossible. There were no outings to the zoo or circus. Leaving Arlene with a teenage baby-sitter for any length of time was unthinkable. Arlene might go into convulsions at any moment.

Nights were always the worst. Occasionally Regina had an earache, flu, sore throat or even a nightmare. These would hardly be noteworthy nights in a normal family, but then we were not a normal family. Regina's cries of, "Mama, Daddy, I don't feel so good," pressed Al into action. I'd shake him awake and he'd stumble out of bed and through the living room to Regina's room off the kitchen. While I fed Arlene, Al rocked and comforted Regina. I still remember walking into Regina's room to find the two of them asleep together in her big, wooden rocking chair.

"I know of people with healthy children who have a worse life than we did," he recalls. "We had love in our family," he says with tears in his eyes. "We just did what we had to do."

One April morning when Arlene was almost three and Regina almost four, as I bent over Arlene's crib, a stab of pain knifed through my back. When the pain hit, I gasped for breath and rested momentarily against the crib rail. Somehow I got through the day. By nightfall the pain was worse; I could hardly straighten up. Then it happened. I'd just finished Arlene's evening feeding and crib check. As I leaned over the crib, a searing pain shot up my spine. Crumbling to the floor, unable to get up, I called Al. Even with his help, I couldn't stand. The piercing pain was too much to bear. I remained on the floor, propped against the crib. Al, despite my loud protests and tears, called our family physician, Dr. Albert Simms. I prayed the pain would go away before the doctor arrived, or if not, that he could give me something to get me back on my feet as soon as possible. I had to keep going. I had to take care of Arlene.

With one look, Dr. Simms said I needed to go to the hospital.

He'd call an ambulance immediately. "No! No!" I protested. I cried. I couldn't leave my sick child! Arlene depended on me. Didn't he know what this would do to her? Only after our next door neighbors, Dr. Marshall Rowdabaugh and his wife, Louise, arrived to stay with Arlene and Regina did I agree to go to St. Joseph's Hospital. Marshall was an anesthesiologist and Louise was one of my best friends. I could entrust the care of my girls to them.

X-rays showed I had ruptured a disc. Apparently the condition went back to my pregnancy with Arlene, that slight pain I had felt in my back. Everyday bending and lifting made it steadily worse. The prognosis: immediate back surgery. Dr. Leroy Miller, a respected neurosurgeon, was called in to perform the laminectomy.

I spent the next ten days in the hospital worrying, wondering and waiting. Mama went to the house each day to take care of the girls. Papa would bring her at nine in the morning. She'd stay all day and after washing the dinner dishes, she and Papa would go home at nine in the evening.

Al visited me several times each day, assuring me that things at home were fine, but I still felt isolated and cut off. From my bed at St. Joseph's, I remembered the October night three years earlier when Arlene was born in the maternity wing just a few floors away. How was Arlene ever going to manage without me?

The nurses listened with patient smiles as I protested that I had to go home, that my sick child at home needed my care and feeding. My God, what if she should die while I was here in the hospital! Desperation turned to fear and panic. I had to will the panic away and pray everything would go right until I got back on my feet. Many times I imagined myself simply walking away from the hospital and the doctors' orders be damned.

When I was released, the doctors insisted I do no more lifting and implied Arlene should be institutionalized for my health. When they asked if I clearly understood the consequences if I continued to lift heavy objects, I meekly nodded yes. But even as I was wheeled from the hospital entrance to our car where Al waited, I knew what I would do, regardless of what it meant. Immediately I went back to my old routine of lifting and bending; Arlene was more important than my health.

CHAPTER FOUR

Birth in the Morning Light

 AMID the continuing stress and inner emotional turmoil, my trusted pediatrician, Dr. William Woodard, encouraged me to have a third child.

The struggle of everyday routine, the lack of freedom other families enjoyed, the constant fear that my inattention might lead to suffering or even death for Arlene, Al's worries about our finances, my concern for Regina—all these things weighed heavier and heavier as the months and years passed. And now another child? Dr. William Woodard had been our pediatrician since Arlene was six months old; she was now almost four, Regina, five.

After we had returned from the devastating Denver trip, I knew I couldn't possibly stay with Drs. Smith and Jones. Their philosophy and care of Arlene differed from mine too greatly. I began immediately to look for a new pediatrician. Dr. Woodard came highly recommended by family friends. At our first meeting, he examined Arlene, then quietly studied her charts and case history. Then he turned to me and said, "I'll do anything and everything to help this little girl."

As a mother, I so desperately needed to hear those words. He probably knew I was hoping for the impossible, but he didn't say so, and more importantly, he was kind and offered concern and understanding to me in that time of heartache and depression. With the frequent visits to his office, the relationship went beyond that of doctor and patient to one of a trusted ally in our battle against the odds that surrounded Arlene.

Dr. Woodard was one of about a dozen pediatricians in Albuquer-

que in the mid-1950s. He came to Albuquerque from his native Tuc-
umcari, in eastern New Mexico. His family were homesteaders. It was
a hard land to face, made harder by the economic crisis gripping the
country. The Great Depression had taught him hardship, heartbreak,
and sorrow, though his was of a different sort than I was facing. But,
possibly because of this common bond, he became a friend and confidante, and we trusted him.

As Al and I sat in Dr. Woodard's office, he suggested it would be best
for everyone if we had a third child. Dr. Woodard was candid as he
told us both what we already knew in our hearts—that Arlene could
die at any time and most likely would never live beyond the age of
eight. In all fairness to ourselves and Regina, we should have another
child.

Listening to him, I found my mind wandering as my eyes focused on
a spot on the wall behind him. "Oh, great," I thought, "the man has
lost his mind. And I must be losing mine, too, to sit here and listen
to this. Isn't my life complicated enough? I should have a third child?
And what's more there are no guarantees that Arlene's sickness won't
occur again."

Bringing myself back to the man in white, I focused again on
Dr. Woodard. He went on to say that in just the few years since
Arlene's birth, we were learning that her condition might not be related to anything hereditary. It seemed that I now really had a choice,
one I never thought I would have. Did I want another child?

I certainly didn't have to take his advice. Yet something within me
wanted to have another baby; something within me wanted to take
the chance. And maybe, too, Dr. Woodard wanted me to put Arlene
in proper perspective. I couldn't continue to live my life for one child
when there was a healthy child who needed my attention, too. Perhaps a third child would enable me to let go, to put all of our lives
back on a more sound footing.

Eight months after that conversation with Dr. Woodard, I was
pregnant. Emotionally and psychologically, it was the most difficult pregnancy of my life. Each time I'd think of the baby I was carrying, I would look at Arlene, resting helplessly in her crib, forever
diapered and bottle-fed, forever my infant. At times I thought I'd lose
my mind with worry.

It was the longest nine months of my life. Despite Dr. Woodard's assurances, I worried Arlene's condition was hereditary. After all, hadn't her doctors been wrong before? Those were, of course, the days before amniocentesis and fetal monitoring. And against doctor's orders and my own better judgment (had I allowed myself to think about it), I continued to do my usual amount of lifting and carrying. I tried to ignore the nagging thoughts that warned me against such strenuous activity because of my bad back and my pregnancy. Instead, I shoved those thoughts into the farthest recesses of my mind, discounting the warnings as old wives' tales, and praying to God that they were just that—old wives' tales.

On the night of September 19, 1960, I started having contractions. Determined not to go to the hospital, I sat in the Rowdabaugh's kitchen, trying to explain to both their satisfaction and mine why I couldn't have another baby at night. Time and again I had said I couldn't have another night baby. The memory of Arlene's night birth was too vivid.

So in the midst of contractions, I kept repeating to myself, long after I left the Rowdabaugh's and through what seemed like an endless night, that I simply could not give birth to another child at night. I knew if another baby of mine was born at night, it would be my undoing. By some sort of inner strength, I held out until the morning light of September 20th. Bright and early, Mama came to stay with Regina and Arlene, while Al and I made the three-mile trip to the hospital.

Al sat calmly in the waiting room, and if he was worried, he didn't let me see it. I drew from his strength. After I was wheeled into the labor room, it was only about an hour before I was taken into the delivery room.

At my request, I had only a saddleblock, and once again I heard what was going on around me, bits and snatches of conversation exchanged between the doctor and nurses. I picked up from them that they were worried for me.

"Is everything all right?" My question seemed to beg for an answer.

"Everything is fine, Mrs. Arrigoni," the doctor and nurses assured me, and I struggled to believe them.

At 10:30 in the morning, my sweet Annette was born. She was big—eight pounds, twelve ounces. Her head was covered with fine, black, curly hair. Her eyes were clear and dark brown. Her complexion peaches and cream. She was beautiful, healthy, and absolutely perfect!

As a precautionary measure, Dr. Woodard prescribed a special Similac formula (non-lactose based) for her while she was in the hospital. Even if there was no indication that Annette was allergic to cow's milk, we felt better about being cautious because of what had happened to Arlene. And once Annette was home, we switched her to goat's milk.

As Annette gained weight and grew, I couldn't help watching her development closely—almost microscopically—searching for any tell-tale signs of abnormality. Of course, there were none. Instead, Annette soon became an active, inquisitive toddler, a dynamo of energy. She was not a nap-taker and nothing I did convinced her to rest. That, in turn, ended my mid-day rests. Between her, Regina and Arlene, I was a happy, but nervous and very tired mother. My back was one continuous ache, and I prayed I would not need further surgery.

Regina went off to school at 8:15 every morning. Such a little lady she was. Then my day would be full of caring for tiny Annette, helping her with her bottle, then trying solid foods, and all too soon seeing her very first steps. It was such a joy to see this healthy little girl growing and developing so fast. It was at moments like these that I blessed Dr. Woodard for encouraging us to have a third child.

But between caring for and playing with the new infant there was the perpetual, continuing care of Arlene, which of course continued night and day. I talked to Arlene as though she were a silent, adult companion, telling her everything I was doing with Annette and how other things in my life were going. I always thought she understood so much more than she could ever tell us. It wasn't long, of course, before Annette understood almost everything I was saying to Arlene. She must have been about two years old. I remember the day. I realized that tiny Annette could understand better than her bigger, older sister, that she had surpassed her already. Annette was weaned and Arlene wasn't. It was a day I will never forget. I reminded myself that Annette was beginning to understand in the usual way we mean understand. She knew the words and most of their meanings, but I will always believe that Arlene understood with her whole being, her heart, in a very special way I will probably never be able to explain.

But the little daughter catching up to the much bigger sister was a turning point for me, as I look back. I think it brought me closer to realizing that the time was coming near when I could no longer handle Arlene's needs all by myself.

Regina was doing well in school and her teachers told us she was a delight in class. This was a relief to Al and me, but especially me, as I had worried my attentions to Arlene were affecting Regina. I worried that she would feel that we loved her less, that perhaps she felt neglected.

Regina sometimes brought her young friends home to visit, even though our house was like a nursing facility in many respects. We have always been so proud of Regina for her acceptance of Arlene. We felt she was always fond of her first sister, even during her very young years. She never seemed embarrassed by Arlene's inability to respond, at her being so different from Regina's other friends and their sisters.

During these years, I rarely left the house. Regina was seven, Arlene was six, and Annette two when I finally admitted to myself that I needed more help in the house. I could not ask Mama for more help. She had done so much already and now found she was busy helping my sister Louise with her five children. That admission was a long time coming and difficult to make. It meant I would have to relinquish my daytime care of Arlene to someone else. It meant admitting I couldn't do everything. I felt I would be letting Arlene down, yet, I knew it was the necessary and right choice.

The idea of daytime help started germinating after Annette was born. After all, I now had three children. Things were getting more complicated and doctors continued to say that sooner or later I wouldn't be able to lift Arlene—not only because of her increasing weight, but also due to my deteriorating back. I could no longer lift Arlene to get her from her wheelchair to the bathtub and then back out of the tub. Soon, I realized, I would not have a choice. The only alternative would be to institutionalize Arlene.

But for now I still had one option—to get help to care for her at home. I wanted someone special, someone who was able to love Arlene as I did. I tried a number of women, one my sister had used to babysit for her children. I used her briefly for night sitting, to give Arlene her bottle. But she and others didn't work out for one reason or another. Some were too impatient and abrupt; others lacked a loving touch.

One day an Italian friend of the family called. Charlie Mayo was the parent of a severely disabled child who had just died. The death had left the woman who had been the child's nurse without a job. He remembered my search for a woman to help with Arlene and wondered if I would be interested in interviewing Antonia Ramírez, a native of Mexico. "She speaks no English," Charlie added as an afterthought.

Charlie's call turned out to be an answer to my prayers. He brought Antonia to our house the next day for the interview, but I use the word "interview" loosely. Communication was something else. She didn't speak English; I spoke limited Spanish. So, after a few unsuccessful attempts, I tried Italian. I speak Italian fluently. It was the only language my parents had spoken at home when I was a child. It worked! The similarity between Spanish and Italian was close enough for us to communicate. Words that didn't translate readily into either language were handled with hand gesturing, of course.

Antonia was a dark-haired, heavy-set woman in her mid-fifties. On her first day with us, without hesitation, she went to Arlene's crib, swept her up in her arms and cradled her next to her heart. Antonia's eyes filled with tears as if remembering another baby, probably the Mayo child. She murmured tender words in Spanish, then began to cry, tears rolling down her cheeks. She wiped them away with the back of her hand, but more came. As I watched silently from the doorway, I, too, began to cry. They were tears of tender joy, for I knew I'd found someone who'd love Arlene as much as I, someone who would soothe her pains, someone who would appreciate her for who she was. I hired Antonia immediately.

Later, I learned Antonia was raising five children alone. Her husband had walked out on her one day, leaving her destitute in this foreign country. Unable to speak the language, she could not find work. She had come by her experience working with handicapped children through her own young son, Luis, who was born with a club foot and severely deformed hand. If Antonia was an answer to my prayers, Arlene was an answer to Antonia's prayers. After the Mayo child died, Antonia had prayed she would find another sick child to care for; it was the only work she knew.

Caring for any disabled or sick child is hard work, physically and emotionally. I knew what Antonia was going through and I empathized with her. Together we laughed and cried. Under those circumstances, she did not stay outside our family circle long. Everyone was quick to adopt her and she adopted us. We became her second family—her daytime family. It's a rare person who has a big enough heart to accommodate two families, but Antonia was one of those precious people. Every day, she made the transition in the morning to our family, and at night she walked the five blocks back to the bus stop and went home to her own family.

Hopeless situations often breed desperate measures. Just as our love for Arlene sent us bouncing from doctor to doctor trying to find a cure, Antonia's love for Arlene sent her seeking cures through natural herbs and *curanderas*, local women who practice *curanderismo*, the ancient Spanish folk art of healing with medicinal herbs and natural remedies. I was willing to try anything; perhaps where modern technology stopped, folk medicine would begin. When these measures failed, too, Antonia was inconsolable. Her faith in her religion and her culture had been shaken.

I felt for her. I took her hand and held it tightly, trying to comfort her as she cried. "Don't worry, Antonia, things are going to be fine," I said quietly and smiled. But inside, my own heart was breaking.

Antonia was totally devoted to Arlene. By nine every morning except Sunday, Antonia was at our door. Her first stop was Arlene's room where Antonia would begin the day by giving Arlene a warm, soothing bath. Bathing, feeding, rocking, and holding Arlene filled Antonia's day. But Antonia could not do everything all the time. Her family needed her at night and she had to leave Arlene to my care.

One thought continued to nag me. Was I giving enough time to my two healthy children? Regina always understood and accepted Arlene's condition, but Annette appeared confused and bewildered as she grew older. A bright, curious toddler, Annette was full of "whys." Why doesn't Arlene grow? Why is Arlene still a baby? Why does Arlene still drink out of a bottle? Why does Arlene still wear diapers? Sometimes she wondered out loud; other times I could tell by the quizzical look on her face as she watched me change diapers or feed Arlene. And, like any young child, she asked the questions over and over.

"Annette, Arlene is not well. She needs special care," I would answer. I did my best to respond in a way Annette could understand, but her curiosity was just a haunting reminder of the questions I asked myself so many times for so many years. Sometimes a child asks questions adults dare not ask, or even ones adults don't know how to answer.

Instinctively, I knew that my hiring Antonia had only postponed the inevitable. I needed to face yet another decision, the question of institutionalizing Arlene. But I didn't want just any institution. It had to be a special place for Arlene.

CHAPTER FIVE

Non Devi Mai Pedere la Speranza
(You Must Never Lose Hope)

 BY THE FALL of 1961, when Arlene was five, she had outgrown her special wooden crib. She was thirty-five inches long and weighed forty-five pounds. Her crib had been custom-designed by a close friend and retired professional carpenter, Marco Donati. The mattress was built so that it was waist-high and I wouldn't have to bend over, risking further damage to my back. Since the crib rolled easily through doorways and down hallways, I was able to move Arlene into the kitchen when I was working there or, at night, into the living room when we watched TV. This way she was always with us and a part of our family life.

The wooden crib was replaced with a chrome hospital-type bed. It wasn't as mobile as the wooden crib, so Arlene now had a wheelchair in which, propped, braced, and belted, she was pushed from room to room. By this time Regina was in first grade and in Brownies; Annette was two and a whirlwind of energy. Antonia was still my godsend, helping throughout the day.

Despite Antonia's indispensable presence, I nursed the growing worry that someday I wouldn't be able to lift Arlene. It might happen during one of those frantic emergency runs to the hospital or during a simple diaper change, and, too, I knew as I got older, my back, already weakened by surgery, would simply give out. It was inevitable. Soon I would have to make new provisions for Arlene—as much for her sake as for Regina and Annette who were being deprived of normal child-hoods. The psychological tug-of-war was wearing me down. I was continually forced to choose between my healthy children and my sick child. Too often Regina and Annette lost out.

Unlike her friends, Regina didn't have a mother working with the PTA. I never got a chance to be a Brownie leader, attend school plays and other performances. These were attended by Al or by no one from our family. Other housewives have friends by the score: neighbors, club friends, or mothers they meet in the usual routine of shopping, taking children to the park, and at church functions. I had none of these experiences. My single outing was to the six o'clock morning mass on Sunday. As busy as my life was, day and night, I wasn't aware of what I was missing. Though our contacts were few, I fondly remember the visits for coffee of my neighbor Louise Rowdabaugh. She was a piece of the outside world, a touch of friendship. And another neighbor I'd occasionally visit, Vestel Tunnel, had made some lovely dresses for Regina.

Now, years later, I realize how hungry I had been for companionship. So much so that I feared I had turned my oldest daughter into a little adult far too early in her life. Because I was so house-bound for so many years, Regina became my best girlfriend.

She was such a good daughter, sometimes I think too good. She didn't have a conventional childhood, anymore than I had an ordinary young mother's life. She tells us she believes she had a wonderful childhood, but to this day Regina takes responsibility seriously. She is a wonderfully caring, nurturing adult, but I think perhaps she's too serious about things.

Adults liked Regina as a child, because she related to them as an adult would. "Very grown up," they would say. Even now I rarely see Regina laugh and she never acts silly and playful. I blame myself for this. She was much too young to bear those heavy burdens.

Yet both Regina and Annette tell us they have happy childhood memories, and I give a lot of the credit to Al. He would play both mother and father to his healthy daughters, taking them places and spending time with them whenever he could. For example, every Halloween he was the one who escorted the girls all around the neighborhood, while I watched over Arlene.

I recall many Sundays in the Sandia Mountains when he took me and the girls inner-tubing at a place called "The Bowl." I remember it as being dangerous. It's a section of the east side of Sandia Mountain, on the way to the ski slopes. Al and the girls would climb up the hill and slide down until they were tired out. Of course, Arlene and I watched from the car during these outings. In good weather we would go to Doc Long's campground and place Arlene near the fire as we all had a great picnic. Then we would sing our favorite songs (especially "I'm Looking Over A Four-Leaf Clover"), and we would inevitably eat too much. Every year we had birthday parties for Regina and Annette at our home. They would invite their friends, and these were some of the most festive times that our house saw each year. Those are fond memories.

Perhaps our happiest moment was the day Arlene was confirmed, a Catholic rite of full participation in all Church sacraments. Al asked the pastor of Our Lady of Fatima if Arlene could be confirmed with the other children. He was stunned when the priest said no because he thought Arlene would disrupt the other children.

Al called the Archbishop of Santa Fe, who was to preside at the ceremony. He immediately agreed to our request and understood our desire to have God's love and blessing offered to all His children in the upcoming public ceremony. Arlene looked wonderful in her dress and hair-ribbon when she was confirmed. She behaved perfectly and didn't make a sound. My sister Louise was her sponsor.

By the time Arlene was five, I had come to a certain peace about her. My mother and father were the biggest help in this, because we would talk for hours as I struggled with the questions, "Why me? Why did this have to happen to Arlene?" I can still hear Mama and Papa saying, *"Non devi mai perdere la speranza."* In Italian, this means "You must never lose hope."

I couldn't have managed without Noni, as the children called my mother, and the solid support of Nono, my father. Arlene especially related to her grandfather. He loved her enormously, and she seemed to know that and responded to him whenever he came to her. When Mama arrived every morning at nine o'clock after Papa dropped her off, she would hold my hand and help me accept God's will. She would say, "God has sent us Arlene for a good reason." Slowly, she helped me see beyond my concerns so that I might see what was best for Arlene and eventually aid other families with special-needs children.

Just as my healthy girls' lives were not conventional, Arlene's world was unfairly limited by her surroundings. The house was too small for her wheelchair. When she tried to manipulate herself, she endlessly bumped, scraped, and crashed into walls and furniture. The narrow confines thwarted her every move. It was painful to watch her frustration.

But still I waited, torn between keeping things as they were and institutionalization, which to me implied abandonment, desertion, quitting, forgetting. How could I ever forget Arlene? She was my flesh and blood, the child I grew to know before she was born. We were more than mother and daughter, we were friends. Despite her inability to communicate in the usual sense, she was incredibly perceptive. She was always alert to my mood shifts. When I was happy, she was happy; when I was sad, she was sad. Because of her inability to communicate, I was her life-line. I thought for her, acted for her, spoke for her.

Yet I wondered: in my desire and attempt to be selfless, was I actually being selfish? So I rationalized and realized that I needed round-the-clock help. Antonia was invaluable during the day, but the nights were long. From five each evening until eight the next morning, it was just Arlene and me. Arlene was in need of care tailored to her personal capabilities and twenty-four hours a day I couldn't provide what she needed. I had to doze off sometime. I couldn't do any more for her. Arlene needed more out of life. Annette, Regina, and Al deserved more of me.

More and more I found my thoughts turning to the idea of placing Arlene in a home for severely disabled children. Being a Catholic and having spent twelve years at St. Mary's School, I pictured a home run by Catholic nuns. A religious order would provide the type of care I could feel comfortable with. Nuns are dedicated women who do not balk at the duties and chores involved in caring for a medically fragile child. They seem to have an inner strength, often reaching beyond the limits of human endurance.

I realize that we accepted life the way it was. Had we not all accepted the whole package—the ordinary as well as the extraordinary—our lives would have been chaotic. Living with one ear always cocked and one eye always open became the norm for our family, and we accepted this. I think our acceptance was the cause of our happiness.

Finally, comfortable and secure with my vision of a nursing home run by Catholic nuns, I set out to find one. I was shocked and disappointed none existed in Albuquerque or New Mexico. Heartbroken, I was forced to revise my thinking. Reluctantly, after a long and emotional personal battle, I agreed to some other institutionalization. But it would be on my terms. I tentatively made inquiries about the nearby state-run institution for the severely handicapped. I knew I had to start some place. I was grasping at straws, groping for someone who would take care of my little Arlene.

One morning in September 1960 Al and I decided to tour the state facility. We headed south along the Rio Grande. As we drove up the tree-lined driveway, onto the well-kept grounds, my heart was filled with hope. Surely a place that tended its grounds so nicely would tend to its patients and residents equally as well. A brief introduction and interview with the superintendent left me only mildly apprehensive. Then we began our tour.

As we started down the hallway, my nostrils were assaulted by the smell of urine; it permeated the air. The surroundings were dirty and dank. The thought of my Arlene here made me physically ill and terribly sad. Some older children with sunken, lifeless eyes and pasty-white skin sat quietly near their beds. There was no interaction and no stimulation. Other children rocked back and forth in corners, drooling. They seemed to be wasting away. There were tiny infants in cribs with severe hydrocephaly, their heads as big as their bodies. No one smiled. In spite of their condition, I longed to hold these children and love them. Held and stroked with loving care, even these children would respond. Arlene with her eyes so veiled was more alive and happier than they. The children seemed so utterly hopeless, so unloved, so abandoned. Had any of these children ever known love? Would they? My heart cried out to them.

I wanted a place that would be cheerful and bright for my angel! Instinctively, I knew a state-run institution was no place for Arlene.

When Al, the superintendent, and I returned to the office, Al candidly asked him, "If it were your child, would you put him or her here?"

The man's answer was a quiet and honest, "No."

"And neither will I," Al's answer was angry and emphatic.

The tour had been devastating. I cried all the way home. Al made a vow. He would build a special room at home, equip it for her, and hire a twenty-four-hour nurse if that were necessary to create an acceptable residence for Arlene.

We could neither eat nor sleep that night; the conditions we'd seen affected us deeply. While lying in bed, unable to even doze, I swore I would go to any length and do anything in my power to get the kind of nursing home I envisioned for Arlene. A place that was clean, spotless, and beautiful. But how could I do that? It all seemed so impossible. I didn't even know how or where to begin. All I knew was our little angel deserved a special place. And she would have it.

With that thought, I closed my eyes for a brief nap before Arlene's next feeding. In my heart I knew if such a place were to exist, Al and I would have to create it; it was up to us and us alone to establish it. I began a dream.

CHAPTER SIX

Dreaming, Then Doing

IN THE HARSH light of day my plan seemed so fragile and full of holes. Who were we to undertake the building of a nursing home? We had no large reserve of funds, no fund-raising experience, no knowledge of hospital administration. We were only two people, the mother and father of a disabled child. By day, I shelved the plan. But at night with her in my arms, I dreamt of a loving home for her and other children like her. The idea had a life and spirit of its own.

One night in the fall of 1961 as I sat feeding and rocking Arlene, looking at her beautiful face with its clear, soft complexion, her curly, brown hair and into her veiled, sightless eyes, the tears of pity started to flow. Then just as suddenly, I stopped crying. Vehemently, I vowed to do it. We were going to build the nursing home; we were going to do something for her and other children like her.

The next morning, after Al had gone to work, and with Antonia taking care of Arlene, Regina in school, and Annette preoccupied, I fortified myself with some inner strength and picked up the phone. On an impulse I dialed the number of the Carmelite Nuns located in Albuquerque's South Valley. I knew these nuns to be a cloistered order, devoting their lives to prayer. I recognized the call for what it was, a long shot. A very long shot. But I thought, maybe, just maybe, these nuns would like to get out and do something on the outside. But the Carmelites were not about to change their cloistered ways for me, that day or any other. Quietly, the mother superior listened to my story of a need for a nursing home for severely disabled children. Then she referred me to the Dominican nuns, an order known for their hospitals and professional nursing abilities.

In Albuquerque, the Dominican nuns operated Nazareth Sanatorium, originally a tuberculosis hospital. In 1961 there was no longer a need for a tuberculosis sanatorium in the community, and the institution became a psychiatric care hospital. In addition, the Dominicans staffed a church and school, St. Therese Little Flower Church on North Fourth Street. The mother superior at the Carmelites suggested I call Sister Therese at the convent. I did just that.

The woman on the phone had a soft, pleasant voice, the kind I was so used to hearing as a child in Catholic school. Her manner encouraged me as I launched into my story. Finishing my last sentence, I waited, holding my breath. There was silence. Did she think I was some sort of nut, someone driven to the lunatic fringe by the enormity of the problem? Suddenly, the silence was broken. She had only been thinking, gathering her own thoughts for a reply.

"I think it's a good idea, but you should call our mother general, Mother à Kempis, in Kenosha, Wisconsin." She gave me the number.

I didn't hesitate, quickly writing it on a handy wide-lined piece of Big Chief tablet paper between the childish scrawls made earlier by Regina, who had been practicing her name. The notation reads: November 9, 1961, at 12:15 Mountain Standard Time, I called Mother à Kempis at St. Catherine Hospital in Kenosha.

It was my third call of the day. My storyline was getting a little smoother each time I told it. I seemed to gain confidence with the retelling. I spoke with Mother à Kempis for fifteen minutes about my search for a place for Arlene, of my special dream for my little girl, and of what kind of place I wanted. Another silent pause—this time a long distance one. Again, I held my breath.

"I will be in Albuquerque in about six months to review my missions," she said. "At that time, let's try to get together. I'll call you when I arrive."

I was ecstatic. I concluded my end of the conversation by saying, that I would do everything possible to have a hospital ready for her and her sisters to staff. As I put down the phone, I felt more hope than I had for months. I was euphoric; then, reality intruded.

"Okay, Rena," I told myself. "You've rattled on and on. Now you'll have to show her you're serious about this, that you're a doer and not just a dreamer."

But how could I prove my determination? Well, first, I needed the backing of the community. I needed some responsible, influential civic leaders to back me up. In five months I had to get them together and show Mother à Kempis we meant business. Now, where would I start?

Being a native of Albuquerque, I knew the names of most of the prominent people of the community. Many I knew personally, so I sat down and drew up a list of people who I hoped would be willing to share their talents and help make my dream a reality. I wanted an entire "foundation" behind children like Arlene, who so desperately needed good people to stand watch over them.

I created a list. The first name I wrote down was Emmanuel Schifani, a first-class mover and shaker, great fund-raiser, and president of Springer Corporation, one of New Mexico's largest companies.

Next I added Peter McCanna, a long-time family friend and an associate of Al's at the P. F. McCanna Real Estate and Insurance Company.

Then I included Jack Craig, a personal acquaintance of ours and a close friend to then Archbishop James Peter Davis of the Diocese of Santa Fe.

I also added John Dwyer, a friend and prominent Albuquerque lawyer, because I felt we would eventually need a lawyer's expertise.

I included Bill LaPine, another family friend, for his accounting abilities.

I listed Dr. Woodard as our medical director because he had taken such fine care of Arlene.

Finally I added Benjamin Raskob, a nationally known philanthropist.

At last I had on paper the first board of the fledgling New Mexico Foundation for Severely Retarded Children. I listed Al and I as members, too.

I think I selected all men for that original Board of Directors because in those days only men had the power to get things done. In later years, we added some wonderful women, but back in the sixties, I was the only woman among all the professional men. And Al's ideas were behind everything I did. He helped me set priorities, and he had brilliant, but always practical, ideas on "how to get there from here." His work schedule was always very hard, so he had to leave most of the "doing" to me.

"Rena is a great promoter. She was really good," Al recalls. "She stayed behind the scenes a lot of the time, and got done what she needed to get done—one way or another. She always stayed on course," he says about those early days. "I don't know how she did it."

Whispering a quick prayer, I started calling each person on my list. I personally talked to all but Ben Raskob. My cousin, Theresa Menicucci, offered to call him and arrange a meeting. She had met him and felt he would know her name and take her call.

Perhaps it was an idea whose time had come. Or maybe I had help from a higher power that day. No one refused me!

To each I explained my story, more briefly this time because everyone who knew Al and me knew of Arlene. I had never made any attempt to hide her or her problems. I told them about the conversation with Mother à Kempis and suggested that we all meet for coffee and rolls at the gracious old Alvarado Hotel next to the Harvey House at the train station in downtown Albuquerque.

Everyone came but Ben Raskob. I was heartbroken when he didn't appear. Anxiously I watched for him, glancing nervously at everyone who entered the coffee shop. Finally I realized we would have to start the meeting without him. I thought of him as so powerful in getting things done. Later I found out his plane had a flat tire in San Francisco, of all things. His flight was delayed just long enough for him to miss our first meeting. It was the only one he would ever miss.

At the meeting, I set out my goals. I told of checking out nearby facilities and finding nothing available or acceptable. I explained that a Dominican nun was coming out to Albuquerque in a few months. I wanted as many of the board members as possible to meet her, so she would know we were organized and legitimate. After all, we were used to thinking of ourselves as "Little Old Albuquerque" way out here in the desert. I knew we had to really impress Mother à Kempis. I realize now that we were making history with our first meeting on January 14, 1962.

Not wanting to leave anything to chance, I called Mother à Kempis the following day and told her of our first meeting and the distinguished members of our foundation. She asked me to call back February 10, when she would be able to confirm the date of her arrival. So it was on one windy night in March 1962 the board of the New Mexico Foundation for Severely Retarded Children finally met with Mother à Kempis at Nazareth Sanitarium.

I will never forget it. Mother à Kempis was a tall, stately woman in her fifties, with penetrating blue eyes and a kind and quiet manner. I loved her the moment I saw her. She seemed interested and excited to meet and talk with us about the project. Her initial encouragement kept our group together during four long years of meetings at the Alvarado Coffee Shop. Every six months Mother à Kempis came to Albuquerque to check on her missions—church, school, and hospital. Each time she offered more encouragement. Each time, it was the shot in the arm I needed.

There were times when it seemed nothing was possible. Idealism was always stumbling against reality. These were men who dealt daily with facts and figures. They didn't make a move without facts or figures— and I had neither. Now and then Peter McCanna, in real estate and insurance, would shake his head and say emphatically, "No way, Rena! It won't work!" I was the lone idealist—or so I thought. That was when I would steal a glance across the table at Benjamin Raskob. He would give me a reassuring wink. That was the only indication I needed to sustain me. "It will work," I would tell myself. "It must."

Looking back now, it seems such a long time to keep enthusiasm going, to keep these fact-and-figure businessmen interested. I guess there was so much to do that the time went quickly. We were making some progress almost every month, and we got encouragement everywhere we turned. We even began to receive some contributions.

In 1964, after two years, our board was bolstered by the addition of Don Kirby, a philanthropist and former Minnesota banker who helped the regional stock brokerage firm of Quinn and Company expand in New Mexico. He was also the grandfather of a child who had to be institutionalized because there was no loving alternative available to deal with his mental retardation. Don knew first-hand how hard it was on a family to have a severely disabled child and how desolate institutions could be.

Two years stretched into four. Still we made progress. Our neighbors Patricia Simmons and Agnes Maloney were faculty members at the University of New Mexico College of Nursing and often came to our meetings. They contributed much from their personal experience and training. And Virginia Keehan from the University of New Mexico contributed her time in scouting out what "human services" were available to help us. Jack Craig owned land in what was then the far Northeast Heights. He offered the land to the Dominican nuns, and said we would build the nursing home just as soon as Mother à Kempis could provide nuns to run such a facility. We were thrilled by his offer and felt we were, at last, close to having a real facility.

During these years, my family life was very demanding. I had little else in my life but family responsibilities and the slow growth of the Foundation. I feel so fortunate to have had the unwavering support of my husband in both. Our girls were growing up, and today both Regina and Annette say we had a "normal family life." It's true that we went through many things all families face. The girls had the usual childhood health problems, of course. Annette had eye problems, and we ended up at a San Francisco specialist. Like so many young families, we had no extra money to invest for the future. The present was absorbing not only all our energies, but all our capital, as well. And keeping Arlene comfortable and content was an additional drain on our limited resources, as any family with a special-needs child can tell you. For us, though, it was one we were more than willing to make.

My oldest daughter remembers "a hundred" trips to the hospital, when Arlene couldn't breathe or had an especially bad infection. We would all tumble into the car, sometimes half-dressed, and rush to the emergency room. Regina remembers many hours sitting in the hospital waiting room, hoping Arlene would pull through again.

Annette was younger and more athletic, more carefree. Her boy cousins often came to roughhouse with her, and she was always the best athlete among them. She has always been an avid tennis player and skier.

It was scary for my young daughters to constantly wonder whether their sister would make it through another day. We'd always been very open with the girls. It was a tough choice, but we felt they had to be prepared. They knew Arlene was expected only to live a few years. She was to prove all the doctors wrong, of course, but the family lived under the perpetual cloud of her sudden loss. Somehow we became accustomed to it. Regina had come to accept this way of life. It was all she knew. After all, she was only a year old when Arlene was born, so Regina had never known a world without her first baby sister.

Also, during this time, Al was swamped with work but somehow managed to get up at night and attend to Regina who had difficulty sleeping. The flying monkeys from the *Wizard of Oz* had frightened her, and for several evenings she experienced nightmares. Al would tell

Regina "I'm going to take those monkeys and swing them around, and around, and out the window." Then later, with Regina safely in his arms, he sat in the old rocking chair and rocked her to sleep. He'd fall asleep also, and I often found them, under a quilt, the next morning.

Amid the routine of everyday living I often called Mother à Kempis to assure her that we were still working hard to build a faculty for severely disabled children. She would always say, "Rena, we do not have enough available nuns at this time."

We realized for the first time that even if the home was built it would stand empty. There wouldn't be enough nuns to staff it. Her words of encouragement began to take on a pessimistic tone.

"Rena," she'd say, "you better pray that more girls become nuns because until I have them we can't get started."

Ironically, both her prayers and mine would be answered. But not before events took on a new twist.

CHAPTER SEVEN

A Letter From Rome

 IN THOSE THREE years after our first meeting, the board of the New Mexico Foundation for Severely Retarded Children had become close. From an embryonic group of concerned citizens in 1962, we'd grown to include some of the top childcare and nursing professionals in the Albuquerque area. Our common goal and our determination drew us together.

By May 1963 participants included Dr. Alvina Looram, with the New Mexico Department of Health in Santa Fe; Dr. Edythe Hershey of the Children's Bureau Dallas Regional Office; Rudy Hormuth from that organization's main base in Washington, D.C.; Mary Patricia "Pat" Simmons, assistant professor of nursing at the University of New Mexico and a member of the Governor's Advisory Council for the Mentally Retarded; Agnes Maloney, also of the UNM College of Nursing; and Dr. Virginia Keehan, an education professor at the University of New Mexico.

We had many, many meetings and much professional input. Each person voiced his or her own thoughts on how a nursing home for children was to operate. When I was impatient, Al calmed me; when I was discouraged, Mother à Kempis encouraged me. Rudy discussed several types of facilities for severely retarded children, those already in operation as well as those experimenting with new programs.

Slowly plans began jelling and by July 1963, we were calling our proposed facility "X Children's Center" in our records. By September, just two months later, we were referring to it as Casa Angelica. The name was not easily come by, though now it seems only natural. I went through many temporary names, some lasting a few days, such as Our Lady of the Way. I rejected some names because they didn't sound right in my heart.

There was a phrase I often spoke to Arlene, "You are the most beautiful angel in the world." Suddenly, I knew the special place for my special angel could be a home for her only if the word, "angel" were in the name. Her home would have to be a house for angels—for many angels. And so it became *Casa Angelica*, an Italian phrase meaning "House of Angels."

In January 1965, even though it looked as though groundbreaking might still be years away, we decided on Bill Ellison as our architect. He was a respected businessman and close friend and associate of Emmanuel Schifani. Emmanuel convinced Bill to donate his professional efforts to the project.

In April 1965, something happened to bring Casa Angelica closer to reality. It began early one morning with a phone call from my sister, Louise Stein. Louise, whose husband was a banker, reported that it was common knowledge in the banking community that a group of nuns was attempting to purchase property south of Albuquerque in the Pajarito Land Grant area off Isleta Boulevard. The nuns, according to her information, were Italian. They were contemplating using the facility as their United States Novitiate, for young women who wished to become nuns of their order. The location would allow novitiates to study in the U.S. instead of making the long journey to Rome. In addition to the novitiate, the nuns would operate a senior citizens nursing home or "something else." That unspecific "something else" immediately offered a ray of hope. Could these nuns be persuaded to make their mission a nursing home for severely retarded children?

"Why don't you call the mother delegate in charge and talk with her?" Louise suggested. I wasted no time. Immediately I learned the mother delegate was Mother Antonietta Colombo and she was headquartered at Annunciation Church in Albuquerque's Northeast Heights. She was a Canossian Daughter of Charity. Established in 1808, the order was founded at Verona, Italy, by Magdalene, Marchioness of Canossa. Primarily a teaching order, the Canossian Sisters are involved in many charitable endeavors and also work in hospitals, leper colonies and orphanages around the world. By nine that morning

I was on the phone to Mother Antonietta, who spoke with a quiet Italian accent. I began with my typical and now well-used introduction, "You don't know me, but. . . ."

By eleven o'clock I was climbing the concrete steps leading to the convent door at Annunciation Church. My knock was answered by a small Italian woman dressed in a black Canossian habit. Smiling, she hugged me warmly. I was totally disarmed; within moments I felt at ease. In addition to her charming manner, I found she was quick-witted with a wonderful sense of humor. But on that bright April morning, she listened quietly to my introduction and informal presentation. Often we lapsed into Italian, a language with which we both felt comfortable.

Mother Antonietta loved the idea of a nursing home for children with special needs, but she alone was powerless to make a decision of such magnitude. She promised to write to Rome, presenting the new idea. We knew those in Rome really wanted a nursing home for the elderly, yet we hoped. Those days spent waiting for Rome's reply passed slowly. The tension was almost unbearable. I fought to restrain myself from calling Mother Antonietta to find out if she'd heard from Italy. These nuns had the location and the staff. Casa Angelica was closer to reality than ever.

To relieve the tension, I buried myself in routine. By now Arlene was nine and weighed almost fifty pounds, though still an infant in most ways. Regina, at ten, was in the fifth grade, and Annette had just started kindergarten. Each day seemed so much like the one before it, yet now they seemed to hold so much promise. Then one day in May the phone rang. It was Mother Antonietta.

"Rena," she began as I held my breath. "I have the best news in the world! I just received a letter from Rome. They said they would be delighted to undertake the project!"

My reaction was one of tremendous relief and uncontained excitement. Even all these years later, I have difficulty describing everything I felt at that moment. Of course, I cried. But for the first time in years, the tears were those of joy and anticipation—at last a home for my angel!

After the phone call, I immediately called a board meeting for that very night at the Alvarado. There with Emmanuel's typical spirit and zeal, he proclaimed, "Let's move it!"

The following day I had the unhappy task of calling Mother à Kempis with the Dominican nuns in Kenosha, Wisconsin. Characteristically, she was silent as she gathered her thoughts. She took the news hard. She was heartbroken and taken aback that we had contacted another group of nuns. I felt her disappointment and felt helpless to comfort her. Then she congratulated me, wished me luck, and added, quietly, she and her order had always hoped to be the ones to build Casa Angelica.

For a while there was a blur of activity. It began when Mother Antonietta phoned one afternoon.

"I'd like you to see where the home will be. Pick me up and I'll show you the place," she said.

That was my first of many trips to the old Spanish-style home in the South Valley, the first of many sixteen-mile drives, trips that continue today. Eventually, I would wear out three cars. I always said if I had a nickel for every mile I drove back and forth, I could have paid for Casa Angelica myself.

But on that first day in 1965, when we drove through the adobe archway and up the quiet, tree-lined driveway, I knew instinctively this was the place for my Arlene. The winding, gravel driveway led past tall, sturdy cottonwoods. It was a place of peace, quiet and strength. I knew it was the answer to my prayers.

The acreage was the rambling estate of the B. Bruce Gardner family. It included a twelve-room house along with fifteen acres of land with 800 feet of frontage on Isleta Boulevard. It is considered one of the most beautiful homes in the South Valley and justly so. In the park-like setting were fountains, trees, patios and a walled courtyard. The home was steeped in history. It had been built in the early 1900s by the late Col. George O. Breece and known as Tapia del Camino Real. Later it was the home of Dr. Harrison L. Brehmer. Although the estate had cost $125,000—a fortune in 1965—it didn't include a stick of furniture. How were nuns and children to live there?

That afternoon, after I took Mother Antonietta back to her convent, I went home and pondered this new dilemma. That night, after Al got home from work, I took him down to see the house. Something in the way of furnishings had to be provided. When we got home, I immediately called a board meeting for the next morning—at Casa Angelica. What a thrill that was, even though I had to ask the board members to bring something to sit on.

The next morning, sitting on folding lawn chairs and even the bare oak floor, the board and Mother Antonietta met in the spacious dining room. Looking around me, I absorbed the idea that this was the first board meeting for Casa Angelica at Casa Angelica. My heart skipped a beat; I smiled to myself. Then I was brought back to reality. Ben Raskob was saying we needed to provide nuns some furnishings. To cover such expenses Ben Raskob went to the telephone and called the Raskob Foundation for a grant of $20,000.00. That day, September 21, 1965, the board allotted up to $12,000 to furnish the home for the nuns. I was put in charge.

I was determined to come in under budget if I possibly could. I knew we had to stretch every dollar. With thriftiness, donations, and lots of volunteer help. For $10,000 I obtained washers, dryers, beds, linens and drapes. We also had to repaint the rooms and fix the plumbing. Within a matter of weeks, we had the convent ready for the nuns.

Initially, the order planned to staff Casa Angelica with two nuns. There were to be Mother Josephine Palmery and Sister Annetta Liata. Upon opening, we were to have four children—my Arlene and three others. In my naiveté, I thought it was now only a matter of obtaining beds, wheelchairs, and linens for the children. Instead I found I was in for a rude awakening—one that almost shattered my dreams.

CHAPTER EIGHT

Financing the First Alfalfa Field

 SUDDENLY, I was thrust into the technical-legal world of government and state regulations. Their big word was *compliance*—and it came with scores of regulations and codes.

The first hurdle was the fire codes. Mother Josephine, Sister Annetta, and I were dutifully in place for our first inspection by the state fire marshal. We didn't just fail, we failed miserably. The inspector pointed aghast at the ancient wooden vigas (ceiling beams) of traditional New Mexico construction; the charming narrow doorways brought a visible shudder and a look of horror. Finally, the antiquated electrical wiring stopped him in his tracks. He was unmoved by the beauty of the historic structure. The initial consensus by fire officials was that the home would have to be rebuilt from the ground up to meet the necessary codes for a nursing home.

Al and I were surprised at all the bureaucracy. "We didn't think we would have so much difficulty," he said. "We weren't expecting so much government involvement in what we were doing. After visiting the State's facility, we thought they would be delighted to have a first class nursing home in Albuquerque."

My heart sank. Had we come this far to have everything fall apart? I couldn't think of anything to do but call an emergency board meeting to present this new and seemingly insurmountable stumbling block. Of course I was incapable of concealing my utter disappointment at the disastrous news. I was close to tears when the board agreed to visit

Casa Angelica the next day to see if it was possible to build an entirely new structure.

The next morning, we carefully studied the grounds. We definitely wouldn't consider tearing up the beautifully landscaped park, but there was an area beyond the cottonwoods to the south. With the practiced eye of a realtor, Al spotted what we later called the "first alfalfa field," facing east onto Isleta Boulevard. The site was large enough for our plans yet close enough to the convent for the nuns' convenience. After all, the nuns would be constantly going back and forth to the nursing home.

After a brief group discussion, Emmanuel, in his typical ramrod fashion which I grew to know, love, and depend on, enthusiastically proclaimed, "Let's move it!" He wanted us all to "get moving" and see what would be involved in our building an entirely new structure. I was thinking, "Where will the money come from? How long will this delay us?"

We got caught up in Emmanuel's eagerness, thank goodness. Al and I really needed this lift to help us overcome our dismay over the fire marshall's report. I was faulting myself. Was I too inexperienced and naive to lead this venture? Should I have asked for more help from Al, in spite of his heavy schedule?

Emmanuel's first step was to contact our architect-in-waiting, Bill Ellison. Bill and Emmanuel had built public buildings, warehouses, office buildings, several schools, but never a hospital or nursing home. For weeks Bill worked closely with me, Al, and Mother Josephine, who would administer the home.

Mother Josephine, a native of Rome, was much too accomplished a person to be described in a few words. She was a world traveler, teacher, social worker, linguist, humanitarian and, most important for us, a trained nurse. Mother Josephine had spent more than thirty years as a Canossian Daughter of Charity when she came to Albuquerque in 1966 to establish the convent, novitiate, and nursing home.

In her early years as a nun, she had been assigned to England. From there she went to Hong Kong, serving throughout World War II and the Japanese occupation. After that she was assigned to Australia, Malaysia, then China. She was in China when the Communists overran the mainland, but her order was allowed to continue working under the shadow of Communist domination. She was transferred back to

London, where she received word from Rome, in 1966, to apply for a visa to the United States. Her next assignment was Albuquerque, New Mexico. I wondered if she knew where it was.

She once summed up her life's experiences by saying, "It is all a very interesting work, a very good work, whether I am teaching in the schools or nursing in the hospital, or helping with the children or working with the people. Where ever I am, I'm always at home." This, then, was the woman Bill Ellison, Al, and I worked with to plan the home.

By early February 1966, Bill submitted a draft plan to the Department of Public Health in Santa Fe for approval. The response was a two-page letter of suggestions and requirements. The isolation room had to be at least 100 square feet; the janitor's closet needed to be completely enclosed; a lavatory was required in the kitchen; and doors opening into the main corridor should be avoided.

It was clear this was going to be a learning experience for all of us. Next came the food and restaurant regulations. By the time we complied with those, we could have opened a commercial restaurant on the Casa Angelica grounds!

When the state officials held hearings on our plans, Bill Ellison, Al and I trekked to Santa Fe. I was nervous. I'd never testified before state officials before.

Al's memory is, "They threw a lot of regulations at us. Maybe it was scary to Rena, but I was used to working with banks, city and county officials, and business people. The state threw more road blocks in our way instead of helping us. They seemed intent on making it difficult."

To questions about the degree of need, I learned to have ready some stock answers. "There is a need," or "It's very important." To questions about the number of retarded children in the community I'd answer, "Oh, there are lots of these children."

I tried to hide the fact that I had no statistics, no figures. I soon came to realize that this all would be easier if I had known enough at the outset to conduct a needs assessment, or get a sociologist to volunteer time to prepare a written study of the needs. But I had never even heard of such reports when I began planning for Casa Angelica in the early 1960s.

We had been told that federal funding through the Hill-Burton Act would pay for half the construction costs on projects such as ours. The application process was so complex and time consuming that we decided it would be more cost effective to move on and not delay.

"No one knew how to handle the application," Al says. "Maybe some good people might have been found who were able to do it, but the delays just weren't worth it. We hoped the state would welcome Casa Angelica, given the problems at their nearby facility. But all we seemed to see were a lot of arrogant bureaucrats."

At times I felt besieged and overwhelmed by the regulations, and forms. Each time I received a new form I'd flinch; I would draw a temporary blank in response even to simple questions. Fortunately, I learned quickly to turn these over to professionals: Pat Simmons, John Dwyer, and Bill Ellison, among others.

By March 1966, we knew that if the state okayed the plans, we would need about $180,000. Where in the world would we get the $180,000 even to begin construction? How long would it take to raise it? I paled at the thought. Another board meeting was planned at the Alvarado Hotel. This time there were only two items of business: the first, take out a loan; the second, begin an auxiliary as a support group. Sitting at our table in the Alvarado, Emmanuel came up with the idea of applying for a loan at the Bank of New Mexico, where he was on the Board of Directors. He and the rest of the Casa Angelica Executive Board would personally guarantee a note for the amount. Ben Raskob immediately agreed and suggested a date be set.

The following week on the morning of March 19, 1966, five board members met at the Bank of New Mexico. Ben, Al, Emmanuel, Peter, and John walked into the Bank of New Mexico to see President Wilfred Clarke. Ben asked Mr. Clarke for a loan of $180,000. Clarke's only comment was, "You have it."

That's the way Albuquerque was in those days and why we loved it so much. And this was an example of the way the community was to receive Casa Angelica and still does.

Ben was the first to sign with his characteristic flourish. Then the others: Al, Peter, Emmanuel, and John, as if they signed $180,000 notes every day. Only later would they admit to some hesitation. "It's not for just anybody that I would march down to the bank and sign a $180,000 note," Peter McCanna recalled. "Only for Casa Angelica. You can't stop and think, 'Oh, God, what will happen if we default.' You shove that thought to the back of your mind. But I always felt things would work out."

It has always been my feeling that Ben, with his background, had a great deal to do with making this happen. He said to me, "Rena, it's only money." Emmanuel, on the other hand, claimed it was inspiration, possibly human, possibly Divine, that led the five of them to sign their names to that note.

A $180,000 loan was taken out for a one year term at 6¾ percent interest. It was a red-letter day. On bank letterhead the terms of the loan were spelled out in formal language. The purpose: "to construct a nursing home for severely retarded children to be operated by the Canossian Daughters of Charity, an order of nuns from Rome, Italy."

When I read the description it seemed stark and impersonal. Our purpose seemed to be lost in those words. Nowhere was there an explanation of the tears and pain, the mental and physical anguish that had gotten us this far. Nowhere was there room to describe the child who had inspired us. Instead there were the words "a nursing home for severely retarded children." It seemed too simple and sterile, so void of feelings, which contrasted greatly to what was going on in our family. Nonetheless, there was a feeling of elation and excitement. What an obligation this loan was. We were getting closer to our dream.

Now that the loan was a fact, we moved on to our second idea for obtaining necessary funds—the auxiliary. Again it was Ben's idea, this time for a group of women volunteers to take care of fund-raising, as well as to oversee the day-to-day needs of the nuns and children. They would be the sustainers. Then, I had no idea what a powerful group this auxiliary was to become. It was the only way we could think of to raise the funds needed by both Casa Angelica and the sisters.

Ben wanted the best Albuquerque had to offer for this project and his suggestion was Anna McCulloch. I knew her from my years at Immaculate Conception Church and Our Lady of Fatima Church. My first conversation with her depressed me because she said she couldn't get involved. She was working with about seven other organizations at the time. After a while I gave up. But only for a while. I would not and could not take "no" for an answer. I called her again. Feeling somewhat guilty that I was hounding her, I nevertheless explained the project was extremely important. Still she gave no commitment. Ben was adamant; it must be Anna McCulloch.

A devoted mother and loving wife, Anna had been brought up to believe one should participate in community and church affairs. For her work within the Catholic Church, she was recognized as one of the outstanding Catholic women in New Mexico and awarded a Papal honor, the pontifical medal Pro Ecclesia Pontifice. These were among the reasons that Anna was the woman Ben wanted to head the auxiliary. And it was up to me to get her for Casa Angelica.

How could I ever face Ben if I failed? Yet the prospect of calling her and once more receiving a "no," was almost more than I could bear. Being a nuisance was more nerve-racking than I had imagined. I took a deep breath, said a little prayer, then sighed and once again reached for the phone. This time I told her of the men involved in the cause. As I reeled off the names, I sensed her interest and suddenly the organization seemed to be taking shape in her mind. It gained substance and legitimacy even as we spoke. I was reminded how lucky I was to have as our board of directors such a powerful group of community leaders. Anna suggested I get together a list of women I'd like to consider for the auxiliary.

My sister, Louise, and I came up with a list of possible charter members, twenty-one women who were close personal friends, family friends, or wives of our husbands' associates. Anna kept her word. When we met a few days later, Louise and I gave her the list.

"You have to get an auxiliary on firm footing," Anna said, as she glanced over the list. "You should have a goal to reach and we need to start right so the organization won't fall to pieces. Casa Angelica seems like such a worthy cause, it has to be done correctly, right from the beginning."

For a month we held two meetings a week, then cut them down to one a week. One of our first tasks was to get the names of all outstanding business and social organizations in Albuquerque and mail each a letter telling them about Casa Angelica and the formation of the auxiliary, the goal we hoped to reach, and, of course, how much we needed their help. We received several responses to help start the auxiliary, but still, these were not enough.

As we continued to comb our Christmas card lists and church rosters for additional auxiliary names, news long awaited came in May 1966 in a letter to Bill Ellison. The New Mexico Department of Public Health had approved our plans for Casa Angelica. Our last hurdle had been crossed and a heavy burden was lifted from our shoulders. We were now truly ready to go. Casa Angelica was five years in the making; we wouldn't postpone its start another second.

I can't describe properly how this affected our family. To say we were happy is so inadequate. At last we felt justified in all our hoping and planning, and, yes, dreaming. Our dreams had not been silly, pie-in-the-sky hopes of a desperate family. The need was there and the home would happen. It was like finding the treasure and being able to say, "See, I told you the map was genuine!" We were hopeful and yet also fulfilled. The work was just beginning, in many ways, but we paused just a bit to celebrate. We set the date for ground breaking for Sunday, May 14, 1966, at 9:30 in the morning.

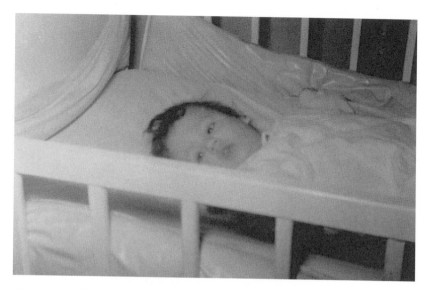

One-year-old Arlene in the crib built especially for her by Marco Donati.

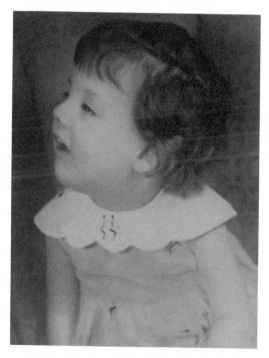

Arlene on her fifth birthday in 1961.

Arlene's sisters in 1962—Regina, age seven, reading to Annette, age 2.

Amerigo and Davina Menicucci, Arlene's devoted grandparents.

Antonia Ramírez cared for Arlene and assisted Rena.

Al, Rena, Regina, and Annette at an Easter Sunday brunch in the mid-1960s.

Mother Antonietta's perseverance made Casa Angelica a reality.

Original members of the Casa Angelica Foundation Board: (*back row, left to right*) Bill Lapine, Al Arrigoni, Benjamin Raskob, and John Dwyer; (*front row, left to right*) Julie Seligman, Don Kirby, Emmanual Schifani, and Rena Arrigoni. Members absent the day the picture was taken were Peter McCanna and Jack Craig.

William Woodard, M.D., provided Arlene medical care throughout her life. He also served as the medical director at Casa Angelica for twenty-five years.

Planning a fund raising event for the Casa Angelica Auxiliary in 1966 are its first president, Anna Mc-Culloch *(right)*, and Louise Stein, sister of Rena Arrigoni.

(above) Architect William W. Ellison's drawing of Casa Angelica.

(top right) Mother Josephine, Rena, and Al at Casa Angelica's ground breaking in May 1966.

(bottom right) Mother Josephine was the first administrator of Casa Angelica.

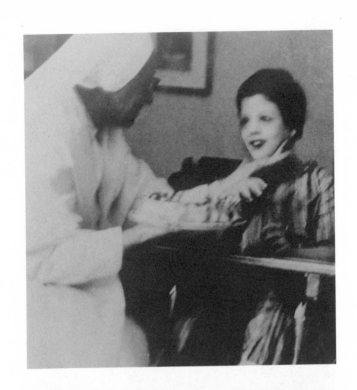

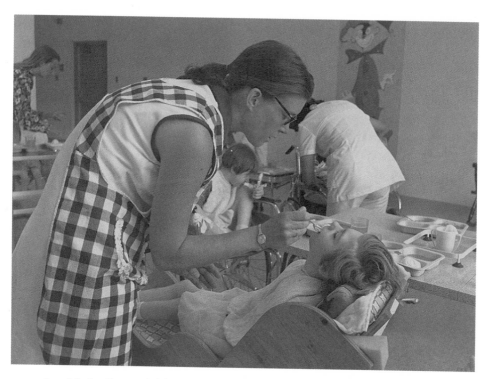

An aide feeding a child at Casa Angelica in the early 1970s.

(top left) Arlene and Mother Josephine at Casa Angelica following its opening in 1967.

(bottom left) Rena and Sister Louise, who took Mother Josephine's place as Casa Angelica's second administrator.

Children enjoying a sunny New Mexico day on the grounds of Casa Angelica.

Sister Louise and three youngsters at play.

Arlene's Memorial Bell.

Sister Louise on the ladder directing the
placement of Arlene's Memorial Bell.

CHAPTER NINE

Ground Breaking on Fertile Soil

MAY 14, 1966, dawned bright and beautiful, one of those sparkling Albuquerque spring mornings when the sun's rays spread over the Sandia Mountains under a cloudless blue sky. Only a slight breeze stirred the leaves. It was a good omen. I so love the sunshine and the morning hours.

The 450 invitations had been sent for the 9:30 A.M. groundbreaking ceremony.

Arriving at the Cristo Rey Convent at 8:30, Al, Regina, Annette, and I were touched by the many bouquets and flower arrangements set under one of the giant cottonwoods near an old garden sundial. The Most Reverend James Peter Davis, Archbishop of Santa Fe, was to preside behind the sundial. Next to arrive were the rest of the Board of Directors and their families for a special Mass in the small private convent chapel, at one time the library of the old adobe house. The Mass was dedicated to the successful completion of the project. As I knelt to pray, I felt confident we'd get the emotional, spiritual, and physical support to see us through this project. Finally, it all seemed possible. My dream for Arlene was coming true. It wouldn't be easy, but yes, it was going to happen.

After Mass, refreshed and invigorated, I went back out into the May morning to greet newly arriving guests, some of whom brought their children. Visitors enjoyed a rare glimpse of the fifteen-acre estate with its spacious lawns, fountains, sundials, a bridge over a small brook, greenhouse, rose gardens and flagstone patios, one with an outdoor barbecue. Vine covered arches and walls completely surrounded the estate. A gate had been cut through a wall to allow the nuns to pass from the convent to the future Casa Angelica. As I walked around to greet our guests, I paused for a moment at the easel next to the sundial under the cottonwoods on the convent's main lawn. Surrounded by bouquets of white carnations and daffodils, the easel displayed the architect's sketch of Casa Angelica. Out of the gloomy darkness a dream was materializing into the bright, shining light of morning.

The design of Casa Angelica was to be a blend of the native New Mexico pueblo style with some practical aspects of modern architecture. Bill Ellison had sketched a flat-roofed, single-story building of cream-colored stucco, which would blend in with local styles and the South Valley's atmosphere. The exterior was to be highlighted with touches of aqua paint on the wood trim under each window, which was also a popular decoration at the time. The same aqua or turquoise tint was to go on the pillars that framed the entryway. The effect was warm and inviting, just what we had in mind.

The board decided that about 7,000 square feet would be necessary to meet all the needs of the core group we expected to live and work in the building. The front wing would house a reception room, some administrative offices, nurses' quarters, a kitchen to prepare the children's meals, with some space for storage and utilities. A small office and laboratory were planned for the staff doctor. At the back of the structure were to be two dormitories, one for girls and one for boys, and behind these an all-weather play area was planned. I think we had thought of everything. I felt a sense of relief mingled with pride at what was about to be accomplished.

Emmanuel Schifani, our master of ceremonies, produced a gold shovel for the ground breaking. As a former City Commissioner, who often presided at groundbreakings, he was able to obtain one of the gold-lacquered scoops to add a touch of official importance to our celebration.

Turning over the first shovel of dark, fertile, river-bottom soil was Archbishop Davis. Casa Angelica was to be operated by the Cannosian Sisters and so would be under his jurisdiction. Next he handed the shovel to Al and me. We turned the soil together. I can't describe the emotion I felt. This tiny gesture was somehow the epitome of our great dream.

When Emmanuel beckoned Mother Josephine, she approached the microphone dressed in her immaculate white habit with a look of joy and anticipation on her face. I watched as this petite, bespectacled nun hesitated a moment. I thought she was not used to being the center of attention.

"We hope to make Casa Angelica an oasis of peace where our special children will find assistance, love, and happiness," she said. Her words put the philosophy of Casa Angelica into focus for everyone present.

Al spoke next. I had no idea what he would say. We hadn't discussed it but his words were moving, intense, and from the heart. I could hardly believe what I was hearing. This tall, rugged, shy man—my rock and pillar of strength—bared emotions I never thought him capable of revealing in public. It was a side of Al I'd never seen before. Gripping both sides of the sundial, he slowly relived his elation and joy at being told once again at the hospital that he was the father of a little girl.

"I saw a beautiful, brown-haired baby, all rosy-cheeked and seemingly healthy, in the hospital nursery. Within days I watched my tiny daughter battle for life in the isolette, jaundiced and struggling to breathe, unable to hold her, unable to help her, and unable to understand why it was happening to her, to me, to us," he recalled.

He told of the trip to Denver with its grim diagnosis of hopeless mental retardation, caused in part by the caregivers we entrusted her life to. Al said Arlene wouldn't give up.

In his words, the magnitude of the moment and the meaning of Casa Angelica was being imprinted on the audience and freshly re-imprinted on me. It was not only to be a home for nameless, faceless, severely disabled children, but for his own daughter, a child whom people had come to recognize, to know, and to love, and who had a name—Arlene—Arlene Arrigoni.

At the mention of her name his voice broke. He paused for a second then haltingly continued. As the assembled crowd experienced a small portion of what he'd felt for ten years, they began to choke back the tears. Arlene became their own Susan, Michael, or Kathy. Handkerchiefs came out, slowly and unobtrusively at first, and guests dabbed at eyes brimming with tears. As he continued, mentioning her name again, tears flowed unabashedly down his cheeks. A drama was unfolding before us. I hadn't known what to expect and this caught me by surprise.

When he'd finished there wasn't a dry eye. The audience knew Casa

Angelica was built on the love and tears of a family who refused to let their child go to a premature death because some doctor thought it best. Arlene was our child, but she could have been the child of anyone there.

Amid the raw emotion my spirits soared for we'd touched a vital nerve. Casa Angelica wouldn't and couldn't fail. I alone, who had cried so many tears, remained dry-eyed. My heart went out to my friends who shared this common bond. Gone were the days when I had been moved to tears because now I was moved to action.

The tentative opening date for Casa Angelica was set for October. It was undoubtedly overly optimistic, but we simply needed a deadline, something to focus on—October 10, 1966. I chose October because I love the month when the cottonwoods and aspens turn New Mexico mountains to gold. Both Regina and Arlene were born in October. And I chose the tenth because it was Arlene's birthday. Casa Angelica would be our birthday present to Arlene. What greater gift could we give her than a life of her own? A special place where the attention and care she needed would be available twenty-four hours a day.

Almost immediately, however, there were delays in starting construction. They were ordinary ones, I was told by Bill Ellison who supervised the on-site progress. Still, they unnerved me. I wanted so badly to make it by Arlene's birthday. A steel strike set back the delivery of the beams. As June came and went, I would have moved heaven and earth to get those beams. Construction finally began in July.

Through the heat of July and August, a small army of men sweated under the hot New Mexico sun in the South Valley. Meanwhile, a dozen women sat in cotton dresses, nylons, and high-heeled shoes in the air conditioned, tree shaded, living room of Anna McCulloch's home near downtown Albuquerque. We were planning the kickoff sherry tea for the auxiliary. While the contrast was stark, our goals were the same. We were all working for Casa Angelica. As the men provided the immediate backbreaking labor, the auxiliary hoped to provide a foundation for the home's long-term financial future.

We considered every kind of event and decided on a tea to introduce potential auxiliary members to Casa Angelica. Hoping to have a large turnout, we planned the tea outdoors where there would be plenty of space on the beautiful Casa Angelica grounds.

On September 1, 1966, the long awaited, much planned auxiliary sherry tea was held. More than 1,000 invitations were sent. As in May, the day dawned bright and warm, under another cloudless Southwestern sky. Tables were arranged under the tall cottonwoods on one of the spacious green lawns of the Cristo Rey Convent—within earshot of the pounding hammers and buzzing drills of construction. Rather than annoyance, they added a note of excitement and anticipation.

More than 500 women drove the twenty miles one way from Albuquerque's Northeast Heights, Southeast Heights, North Valley or downtown. Approaching Casa Angelica, they followed the winding, narrow, two-lane highway through barrios and past 100-year-old farm houses, alfalfa fields and apple orchards. Some came perhaps out of curiosity and for a chance to tour the historic adobe house and grounds. Others came out of a sense of community spirit and commitment to their home town.

That is what our community was like then. Everyone seemed to know everyone else, and there was a civic pride borne of a common interest in seeing that life was good here in Albuquerque. We took care of our own, and we gave generously to things like our symphony orchestra and the poor. We were probably not very different from hundreds of American towns and cities, though of course we thought we were special. The people who ran Albuquerque—the city manager, the stock brokers, the bankers, all the people in responsible positions—knew one another and supported each other's causes.

Albuquerque is a lot bigger now, about half a million, but at the dedication of Casa Angelica in 1966 we were intimate enough to make anything happen because we got behind the causes we believed in. Looking back, I realize I took that togetherness for granted. I had always been part of it. Albuquerque was the only town I knew. Now I realize how very special that time in our community was. Everyone who came that day knew they were going to be asked for some of their time or for a donation, yet they came willingly, even eagerly.

The spark of enthusiasm spread quickly. Anything done with enthusiasm will reap its own rewards, and how Casa Angelica was rewarded! Eagerly, visitors began signing up for various committees.

With the money from the five-dollar membership dues, we bought linens and towels for the nuns. Without them there could be no Casa Angelica. Therefore, our first project was to make the convent habitable. Even though it was only September, some women offered to provide Thanksgiving and Christmas dinners for the nuns or decorate the first Casa Angelica Christmas tree. Others volunteered to patch and mend the children's clothing, to raise funds for washing machines, or to provide transportation for the nuns. Returning home that afternoon, I knew that our first auxiliary membership tea succeeded beyond our wildest expectations.

The construction was a different story. By mid-September, it became obvious that Casa Angelica would not open in October, though the interior work was progressing quickly. Four noted Albuquerque artists offered to donate murals of nursery rhymes and Mother Goose characters for the walls. Those bright moments of unsolicited donations from Kitty Sadock, Ou Mie-Shu, Rita M. Simmons, and Ann Stubbs made time pass quickly.

In addition to my responsibilities surrounding the actual construction and furnishing of Casa Angelica, by December I'd become educated on immigration and naturalization laws. The Cannosian Sisters, who were to staff Casa Angelica, came from all parts of the world. Each required a visa and petition for her entry into the United States. There were interviews with the immigration officer in charge, Mariano G. Islas. With Sister Antonetta Liati coming from Italy, Sister Stella Negri from London, and Sister Concetta Coppe from Brisbane, Australia, it was a hectic time. Applications had to be filled out by the nuns in the countries where they were working, and a separate form had to be filed by officials in the United States. If I had been amazed earlier at the sheets and sheets of forms required at the state level to start Casa Angelica, I could only be astounded by the paperwork at the federal level to staff Casa Angelica.

In January 1967 we received word that the state would make its final interior rooms inspection of Casa Angelica. Bill wanted me there. Nervous and anxious, I walked through the front doors. Smelling the new paint and seeing the spotless walls and new carpeting of the large, cheerful reception room, I was filled with exuberance. Surely our dream was about to come true. By noon the inspection was complete. Casa Angelica was a nursing home.

We quickly began planning an official opening, one befitting a "House of Angels." There would be a Mass and a blessing from Archbishop Davis. We set the opening date: Sunday January 16, 1967. Little did we know that this was also the day of the first ever Super Bowl football game.

Providence again smiled on us. The winter Sunday dawned bright, sunny, and warm. While snow draped the Sandia Mountains to the east and ice clung to the TV towers on the mountain crest, the roads in the valley were dry and the weather balmy.

That Sunday many Americans planted themselves in front of TV sets across the country to watch the Green Bay Packers beat the Kansas City Chiefs 35 to 10. As the legendary Green Bay coach, Vince Lombardi, heatedly paced the sidelines, a small army of Italian compatriots triumphed over a hot stove in the Cristo Rey Convent to prepare a bountiful lunch for the Archbishop, Casa Angelica board members, and families. The lunch was served buffet style in the convent dining room. Fortunately, for many of the men, including the Archbishop, the living room and the television set were close enough to let them pop in for important plays and to keep track of the score.

The Archbishop kept his speech brief. It was just a short walk from the convent through the gate to Casa Angelica's front steps where an aqua blue ribbon was draped. With one quick snip, the ribbon was cut and the ends parted, opening the doors of Casa Angelica to the public. While the men hurried back to the convent living room and the television, the nuns led the women and children on the tour of Casa Angelica.

By late January 1967, the nuns were comfortably settled in the well-furnished convent. The first three children arrived at Casa Angelica, their new home. There was little Beth, tiny Yvonne, and frail Randy. But Arlene was not among them.

Days passed, then weeks. Finally, the nuns politely pressed me.

"Rena," began Mother Josephine, "You've worked so hard for this. Now that it's here, Arlene isn't."

I smiled and turned away. I knew this was coming. The dread had been building inside me, wrenching at my heart. It was time—time for Arlene to go. And now I couldn't let her go.

CHAPTER TEN

Letting Go

AS I FED and bathed Arlene or watched Antonia feed and diaper her, I reminded myself Casa Angelica would be best for my little girl. Wouldn't it? There she would be surrounded by professionals who knew how to read a need and nurture a heart. Still, the thought of turning my daughter over to others tormented me.

A month passed before I came to terms with my thoughts and dealt with them. Just as I was ready to let go, I found out that I wasn't the only one having difficulties grappling with these emotions. Regina couldn't let Arlene go either. At eleven she was just a year older than Arlene, but wise beyond her years. She, who had so wished for a baby sister ten years earlier, who even as a toddler would tug and pull at Arlene's hair in the hopes of getting a response in order to show everyone Arlene was just temporarily ill, she who loved her younger sister dearly, couldn't let her go.

She called placing Arlene in Casa Angelica "losing her." That became the only excuse I needed. I adopted a philosophy that was entirely unlike me, but it suited my needs, "Don't do today what you can put off until tomorrow." It was the first and only time in my life I procrastinated. So while Arlene continued her day-to-day struggle to survive, Regina became an increasingly depressed, sullen child who frequently announced loudly that Arlene should "stay at home."

Several more months passed, and it became too much for me to bear alone. I called our parish priest. If he talked with Regina and explained it was time and best for Arlene to go, perhaps Regina would understand. Was Regina impressed with the priest or his message? Only she knew. I never pried. I only knew she had given in. Now the decision was truly up to me. I had to let go if Casa Angelica was to become her new home. On a cold February night after I had checked Arlene and started back to my bedroom, the resolution came. The following Saturday night, I would make the break.

Saturday morning I broke the news to dear, faithful Antonia. On Monday she wouldn't have to come care for Arlene. It was inevitable; Antonia knew from the day she came to us five years earlier that this moment would come.

"*¡Qué, Arlene!*" she cried as each minute ticked closer to the hour when she, too, would have to relinquish Arlene's care to others. Often throughout the day she would remind me, in her lilting Spanish, that I had promised to drive her to Casa Angelica to see "my angel". Even as I assured her over and over I would, she wiped her eyes with her apron as she fed or cleaned Arlene.

Al borrowed my brother's pickup truck to carry Arlene's things. All day Saturday, the truck stayed parked in the driveway. Despite my bravado, I couldn't steel myself to load it. The girls and Al, even Antonia, stole glances at me, looking for some cue to begin. They wouldn't start until I gave the word.

I felt that I was failing her as a mother. How could I do this to my own child? How could I not care for her? But as I watched Arlene frustratingly navigate her wheelchair through the small doorways in our home, I pictured the beautiful, wide doorways at Casa Angelica. Quietly I nodded to Al. It was time. He began dismantling the heavy institutional crib and loaded the metal pieces onto the truck. As each piece of furniture, even the rocking chair was loaded carefully under the cold moonlight night. I watched through blinding tears.

Arlene nodded sleepily as the girls and I bundled her up and I carried her to the car. We followed Al as he drove the pickup. With Arlene and Annette in the back seat and Regina next to me, we made the silent trip to Casa Angelica. In the hush, I knew why I chose night to make this break. I told myself it would be easier if Arlene woke up in her new world for her new beginning. Subconsciously, I probably couldn't do it any other time. Arlene came to me in the night; she would leave me in the night.

Mother Josephine greeted us at the door. She masked her surprise. "Arlene, you finally got here," she said gently.

Mother Josephine showed Al where to put the bed. As quietly as possible, he reassembled the metal crib, taking care to muffle the clank of metal on metal so as not to wake the other children.

When the bed was assembled, he carried in the rocking chair. Holding Arlene, I rocked her until she was almost asleep. I gazed once more at her beautiful face and curly brown hair then quietly handed her over to an aide, Mary Jane Cuaron.

As we left, Arlene was dozing in Mary Jane's arms. It was a good sign that Arlene had taken so easily to Mary Jane.

The drive home—though it was no longer Arlene's home—was somber. All of us had left parts of ourselves at Casa Angelica.

I stayed awake most of the night crying and pacing the floor. At every turn, I imagined hearing Arlene call for me in her distinctive way. She had been such a part of my life the last ten years that I thought I heard her breathing in the next room.

As I wept, I thought back to the day I first learned Arlene had irreversible brain damage. Tonight was just as sad. Even though I knew Casa Angelica was the best place for her, I felt I had lost her. It was a pain as bleak as death. Though we were only miles apart, it might as well as have been worlds apart. It was a terrible finality. I knew I could never bring her to this home again. If I succumbed to the temptation of a home "visit," I knew in my heart I would never take her back.

For a year after "the move," as I came to call it, I imagined hearing Arlene stirring and moving in her crib, calling for me in her way, asking to be fed, changed, or cleaned. But the call was now answered by nuns and aides at her new home, a house of angels, Casa Angelica.

It was to be her final home.

CHAPTER ELEVEN

Visiting My Angel

 WE WERE STILL very much a family although Arlene was not living with us. If anything, our bonds strengthened. Casa Angelica became an integral part of our lives because it was now the center of Arlene's life.

I made daily trips to visit her. After the girls headed off to school in the morning, I straightened the house, then zoomed down to see her. I'd hurry home about two in the afternoon when Regina and Annette arrived. My mornings were for Arlene, and what beautiful mornings they were. I was free of the daily, nerve-racking tension of life-threatening high fevers and convulsions. The hectic, headlong, high-speed dashes to the hospital emergency rooms were a distant memory. Without the added tensions we enjoyed each other's company. We became close friends. She was my confidante as never before.

Every Sunday after mass, Regina, Annette, Al, and I drove south on the winding road to Casa Angelica. There, as in the old days, Regina laughingly teased Arlene in her familiar older-to-younger-sister exchange. Annette, too young to remember the sisterly bantering, shyly hung back. After the first boisterous greetings, Annette and Regina often folded diapers in the laundry room, leaving Arlene with Al's and my undivided attention.

On Arlene's birthdays we brought cake and ice cream. The whole family, along with the nuns, would sing loud and lusty renditions of "Happy Birthday." Christmas, as every holiday, found the Arrigonis enjoying a double celebration, first at home, then at Casa Angelica.

The nuns claimed Arlene sensed my presence at Casa Angelica when I'd drive up the long, winding driveway. They even asked that I not come during lunch because in her excitement to be with me she'd refuse to eat.

Before and after lunch, I wheeled her up and down the long corridor as I laughed, talked, and shouted hellos to the nuns. Depending on the season and weather, we sat under the cottonwoods or in the quiet lounge near the front entrance. I shared with her the family's comings and goings, her sisters' grades and social events, as well as my innermost worries and fears.

Arlene jealously guarded our time together. If others sought my attention for even the smallest moment, she physically pushed them away as if to assert that this was her time with me! Others were neither welcomed nor tolerated. In that way, our relationship was more demanding than it had been at home. Still, this was a small price for her care and happiness.

Not every day was sunny. Sometimes, I found her enclosed in an oxygen tent, unconscious, her body racked with a high fever and on the verge of convulsions. Despite these episodes I felt confident of the nuns' ability to handle any crisis.

When Arlene was hospitalized at fifteen for severely swollen tonsils, Sister Concetta, a petite, dark-haired, dark-eyed nun who looked like a young Audrey Hepburn, stayed with her around the clock suctioning her trachea. The tonsils were so enlarged Arlene gasped for breath and couldn't swallow even minutely minced food. Doctors first considered a tracheotomy, then agreed on a tonsillectomy, normally a simple operation, which they believed to be only slightly more difficult in her case.

The doctors couldn't have been more wrong. At seven that cold December morning, she was wheeled into an operating room. Sister Concetta, as the doctor had requested, was in her nun's habit cloaked with a sterile gown and her face covered with a mask. As the doctors prepared Arlene for surgery by inserting a tube into her mouth, her jaws clamped shut.

Two hours later, a heavily perspiring doctor emerged from the operating room to tell us it was impossible to operate. Worse, he didn't know if her jaw muscles would ever relax. She might have to be fed intravenously for the rest of her life. She remained under close observation for three days while her jaws remained locked shut. Feeding was done intravenously. Ever faithful Sister Concetta stayed at her side.

After three days she was moved back to Casa Angelica. There Arlene's jaws relaxed. Still the enlarged tonsils remained. In mid-January, Arlene's doctors recommended, instead of risking surgery, an experimental treatment with cobalt to burn out the tonsils.

The treatment required a three-day hospital stay which left Arlene nauseated, exhausted, and physically drained. She lost ten pounds, a drastic drop since she weighed only sixty-five pounds. In the hospital she lapsed into a deep sleep, but the tonsils disappeared, and she began to breathe more easily. Once back at Casa Angelica, she was nursed to health by the loving, vigilant nuns who were molding a special life for our little angel.

I took great comfort in knowing Arlene was well cared for and loved at Casa Angelica, but I still had one main worry: could we pay the quarterly Casa Angelica mortgage?

"What have I done? What have I gotten my family and friends into? Where are we going from here?"

The board members had personally guaranteed the loan. If we couldn't come up with the money every three months, we could be in default on the loan. The bank could step in and take everything. I envisioned Casa Angelica being shut down, the children cast out on the streets, and board members losing their homes—all because of me. Yet each quarter, with God's help, we always found a way to pay the bank.

In 1970 another family medical crisis presented itself. My sister, Louise, who'd been a source of great strength during Arlene's early years, who adored Arlene, and who first thought of the idea of approaching the Canossian sisters, was now dying of kidney failure. Every day before visiting Arlene, I stopped by St. Joseph Hospital to see Louise. My feeble attempts to cheer her often left my nerves so ragged that by the time I reached Arlene, I was ready to cry torrents of tears. On those days Arlene's strength was amazing. This child who'd so often cheated deaths, lifted my spirits. She understood my emotions and responded. A child once branded hopelessly incapable of doing anything offered me solace during my sister's dying.

CHAPTER TWELVE

From Milan to the South Valley

ARLENE'S twelve years at Casa Angelica were the happiest times of her life. She had care twenty-four hours a day, and the loving attention of the nuns. Casa Angelica was her home—her second family.

This second family was headed by the indomitable Sister Louise, who replaced Mother Josephine when the founding sister retired to Australia in 1970. Arlene enjoyed a sister-brother relationship with courageous children like Tommy, Johnny, Luke, and Arnold, all fighting their own personal battles to survive. They were a large, loving, and sometimes boisterous family, which we were fortunate to know and love.

Sister Louise Giugni's path to Casa Angelica began in the tiny northern Italian farming town of Sondrio, nestled in the crown of the lower Alps on the Swiss border. So close is Sondrio to Switzerland that Sister's accent resembled the neighboring Swiss.

In 1940 at seventeen, Louise became a nun and a teacher in the Canossian Order. Twenty-one years later, in 1961, as she prepared to leave from London for a teaching assignment in Hong Kong, the travel plans for her and three other nuns were abruptly changed to a place she'd never heard of—Albuquerque, New Mexico. Her new temporary assignment, she was told, was to be principal of the new parochial school the Order was opening. Once the school got on firm footing, she'd go on to China. This was to only take a year or so.

Sister Louise immediately returned to Milan where she joined Mother Antonietta, Sister Dorothy, and Sister Teresa. From Milan they flew to Turin, Paris, and New York. In New York they asked directions to Albuquerque. Politely, the nuns were put on a flight to Memphis, then to Dallas. In Dallas they again asked, "How do we get to Albuquerque?"

Whether it was the nuns' religious attire or some Texas sense of humor, they were directed to a mail plane waiting to take off.

Sister Louise recalled the final leg with a laugh,"We had no idea where we were going and we began to wonder where this place was that you had to go there in a mail plane. We had paid for commercial airfare. We'd travelled all the way by jet. Yet the pilot put us in seats among his mail bags, and off we flew to the west. I was never so sick as I was on that plane."

Exhausted after twenty-seven hours in the air, the nuns arrived in Albuquerque shortly after midnight on August 17, 1961. As they stepped off the mail plane that hot summer night, two parish priests and a welcoming committee of women greeted them.

"I had no idea how long the women and priests had waited, and I was in no condition to ask," Sister laughed.

Sister Louise had only weeks to organize her teaching staff at Annunciation School. Besides serving as principal, she also taught math. She was at her best in the classroom. She loved to teach and loved to see the light in a child's eyes when he or she grasped a new concept. She loved to see children bloom and grow mentally.

In her nine years in this temporary assignment enrollment grew and the school expanded its physical plant. One day Mother Antonietta broached a new challenge for her. With Mother Josephine retiring, would she become the administrator at Casa Angelica?

"I am a teacher, not a nurse or physician, so I had my doubts," She later revealed. "Nevertheless, I told Mother Antonietta that if she really wanted me there, I would try."

Immediately, Sister Louise immersed herself in the world of medicine and familiarized herself with each child's medical chart until she knew each one's unique problems. The children were not total strangers to her. She had volunteered many weekends and school vacations to feed them and prepare their food. It was then, too, that she discovered her second love—nursing.

"I found, for the most part, nursing requires good common sense, the ability to follow the doctor's orders, loving care, and the ability to think for the patients, to anticipate their needs, because in most cases they are unable to communicate those needs," she explained. "At Casa Angelica it meant thinking for twenty-five children."

The impact of Casa Angelica on the nuns who undertook its challenge was enormous, of course. And it goes without saying that Casa Angelica improved the lives of all the children and families of the children who lived there.

Some of the nuns made changes in the healthcare systems, too. After she had been at Casa Angelica a short while, Sister Louise insisted that a nun accompany any child requiring hospitalization, just as any caring parent would.

"Many times the hospital nurse assigned to a disabled child doesn't know the child well enough to understand why he is not eating his breakfast or why she is whimpering when she's sitting upright in a particular chair," Sister Louise explained.

"I remember one of the times Luke went to the hospital," she recalled. "This was before we began staying with the children. He had a condition that made his bones very fragile, so fragile that even turning over in bed caused them to break and fracture.

"I arrived to find his breakfast tray untouched. The explanation from the nurse was that she had tried, but Luke didn't want it. I tried, and he ate and drank everything.

"At another time, I walked in to find Arnold sitting up in his chair, whimpering and fussing. The problem was his hip bones were rubbing directly on the metal chair. He couldn't explain this; he couldn't point to the problem; all he could do was whimper. The simple act of tilting the chair at a certain angle, relieved his discomfort," Sister said.

The nuns' ability to anticipate and ease the pain made them devoted and loving surrogate mothers to the children of Casa Angelica. At first nurses would slip in quietly to the hospital rooms to observe the nuns as they bathed and fed the children. Soon several area hospitals sent their student nurses and interns to Casa Angelica as part of their regular teaching curriculum. The interns began coming to Casa Angelica to study the long term effects of fetal alcohol syndrome, microcephalus, hydrocephalus, and Low's syndrome, the latter a condition that causes fragile bones.

Both Mother Josephine and Sister Louise believed children needed more than a comfortable bed and loving care. Physical therapy was a vital tool because the one-on-one attention the nuns gave the children produced some of the most dramatic breakthroughs. During this time of play and exercise, the nuns worked eagerly for signs of progress, the children worked to please the nuns, and together teachers and students rejoiced at each new move and every new syllable.

At Casa Angelica Arlene learned to say five words, the only words she ever spoke.

Mom was her first word. To me it was the most beautiful word I had ever heard. Arlene was then twelve. Every evening at five I called Arlene. She came to expect the call and desperately maneuvered her wheelchair toward the office telephone whenever she heard it ring.

"Mama's on the phone," the nuns told her.

"Arlie, say Mom," I coaxed.

"Mom," she'd laugh.

"Arlie," I'd say, giddy with joy, "you're the most beautiful baby in the world."

The second word was *today*.

"Mama is coming today," the nuns would tell her.

"Today, today, today," she repeated, as if it were her own private song.

Baby was her next word. When I called or visited, I told her over and over "Arlie, you're the most beautiful baby in the world."

"Baby, baby," she'd repeated.

Next came *sister*.

One Easter night Mother Ida Nardi was kissing each child and making sure they were tucked in. She had just tucked in Arlene and kissed her, then moved to the next crib. Behind her a voice said quietly but distinctly, "sister."

Mother turned and listened. Was someone else in the room? Again came the voice and the word, "sister" As her eyes rested on Arlene's face, Arlene repeated, "sister." Excitedly Mother Nardi raced to the phone to tell me of Arlene's latest achievement.

Finally, on one sunny Sunday visit when Arlene was about eighteen, she surprised the whole family by speaking her fifth word.

Dad.

Tears rose to Al's eyes.

"She finally learned to say my name," he whispered proudly.

Arlene's progress sparked hope among family, friends, nuns, and doctors. Had she reached a turning point? Perhaps recent medical advancements could help her and others like her. Sister Louise saw these small sparks of learning and was infused with the desire to have the best education for each and every one of these twenty-five special children. Her determination sparked a pilot program, focusing nationwide attention on the educational needs of mentally and physically challenged children.

CHAPTER THIRTEEN

The Story of a Lost Child

ARLENE, of course, was not the only youngster at Casa Angelica. From the initial three residents in 1967, the number increased steadily until twenty-five youngsters lived at Casa Angelica by the end of 1968. I'll never forget the first time I saw Tommy. Even at three he was a charmer. His black hair and dark brown eyes bespoke his Pueblo Indian ancestry. He was born with spina bifida, which caused paralysis below the waist. Because his kidneys were not functioning, he had an ileostomy, a bag attached through an opening in his bladder wall that collected the urine. He'd been brought to the Bernalillo County Medical Center by his parents who felt they could no longer care for him. This is when Sister Louise first saw Tommy.

She was at the hospital with little Maria, a resident of Casa Angelica, who required a hospital stay. Tommy's doctor pleaded with Sister Louise to take the boy home to Casa Angelica. The physician felt he could do no more for the boy. Sister Louise saw a spark of determination, and alertness to the world around him, and the desire to learn. It was such a profound desire that it touched her heart.

"I have no room," Sister Louise lamented as she described the dilemma to me. "He is in every sense a 'lost' child. I have no room and, above all, I have no legal right to just take him." Nonetheless, she began the paperwork to transfer custody. Beginning in 1967, Casa Angelica extended its mission from a private facility to one that cared for children referred by doctors.

Six months later an opening occurred and, with the paperwork completed, she brought Tommy to Casa Angelica. The bond they forged endured for more than fifteen years.

"In those first days, Tommy was a sullen child, unable or unwilling to speak. After she started working with him, he began moving his wheelchair on his own, just short jerky movements, without any particular direction. But at least it gave him a sense of mobility and control, however small, over something in his environment."

"When he was lying down," Sister Louise recalled, "his attention would be attracted by something and he would point. We'd respond by telling him what it was. If it could be moved, we brought it to him encouraging him to touch and feel it."

Amazingly, he started picking up sounds. Before long, he could say a few words, at first simple words and later he was able to form sentences.

"Sister E-eese," he called Sister Louise.

When he was about five, Sister started looking for an educational program outside Casa Angelica. She was sure he could do much more.

"At the same time, his vision began fading. Yet he was demanding more attention, the attention that shows an inquisitive mind; always asking questions, wanting answers. It was delightful," Sister remembered.

The first program she found was a preschool called Esperanza Para Nuestros Niños, which means "Hope For Our Children." Tommy was in the program only six months because, even at the age of five, he was over age. And, by this time he was almost blind.

"It was a great experience for him," Sister Louise recalled. "Though I was using most of my time taking him back and forth to school, it was very productive. Every morning he and I would pile into the station wagon shortly before nine and drive the short distance to the school. I'd unload him and put him in his wheelchair, wheel him into the school and leave. At two in the afternoon, I'd pick him up for the trip home."

"He chattered all the way, asking questions, asking this and that about the car."

"Why are we stopping?"

"Because of the red light."

"Are we stopping because of a red light?"

"No, I'm turning into the gas station."

"What was that sound?"

"That's a motorscooter."

"Are we home yet?"

He was so eager to learn about the world of light around him, even as he steadily slipped into a world of darkness. By the end of June he was totally blind. But the preschool experience made him a different child. We had watched him go from an immobile, silent little boy to an outgoing, active child.

Now, what to do with this bright, gregarious youngster? Sister Louise reminded me of myself as I'd tried to make Arlene's life as fulfilling as possible. Ever determined, she turned to the New Mexico School for the Visually Handicapped in Alamogordo, some 230 miles southeast of Albuquerque.

"Initially, I was told the school couldn't take him because of his many other handicaps: the ileostomy and paralysis," Sister said. "But I invited the nursing director and the program director to come see Tommy at Casa Angelica. During a visit to Albuquerque I showed them a little boy who, though confined to a wheelchair, was alert, playful, and eager to learn. They couldn't have asked for a more willing pupil. There and then they decided that he was accepted. But we would now have to convince 'the others.' By that they meant the people in charge of the dormitories."

As a young nun, Sister had been in charge of a girls' dormitory. She'd dried the tears of homesickness, nursed real and imagined illnesses, and understood the problems, and she wasn't going to let this chance slip by.

"Emotionally, we have come too far. Now we have to go the physical distance," she explained to me one day after the visit. She soon made arrangements to take Tommy to visit the school. On the summer morning they left, she packed two suitcases and put them in the station wagon. Then in went the wheelchair and Tommy.

"We headed south along the interstate, gradually getting into warmer temperatures near the desert valley. On the way we talked about what we would find in Alamogordo. Neither of us had ever been to the place called Alamogordo, which means, "fat cottonwood." We talked of the desert, its heat in the summer and its cold in the winter, of the tiny desert mice, coyotes and owls, the tall yucca, and low clusters of green snakeweed," she said.

"Tommy could hardly contain his excitement and anticipation," she went on. "He understood he was a big boy to be going away to school, but first he must show these people he was a big boy and ready to be away from home."

As they drove up to the main building, Sister explained to him what she saw. "It was a big campus, some one-story and some two-story red brick buildings with white trimmed windows, doors, and wheelchair ramps surrounded by acres of green grass. All under huge, spreading shade trees. The campus was bigger than I had thought. And I wondered, with a mother's heart, if he would be able to find his way around; after all, he was just a little boy."

In their two days at the Alamogordo campus, Tommy won hearts with his even temperament and affectionate ways. Sister Louise instructed the dorm supervisors how to empty and reattach the ileostomy bag. By the end of their stay, Tommy had earned himself a place among the fall students.

Now Sister needed permission from Tommy's parents, whom he hadn't seen in two years. She hoped they could be easily located, and would agree to her plan. From Albuquerque, she and Tommy set out to find his parents at their pueblo home eighty miles to the West. With a few questions and only a little backtracking they were able to find his parents. Their initial reaction chilled Sister Louise.

"No. There is no need for this child to go to school," they argued.

Calmly and patiently, Sister explained how much she loved Tommy and what a bright and eager child he was. She desperately wanted him to have the opportunity to learn. She told about the school and the opportunities that awaited him.

After a hushed silence and an exchange of long looks between father and mother, Tommy's parents reluctantly relented. Confidently, Sister Louise left the pueblo with the precious permission in hand. Tommy could begin his education. It was a hallmark for Sister Louise when she was able to see Tommy off to school. A special bus picked him up in Albuquerque. The driver loaded his few suitcases, then Tommy in his wheelchair, for the trip to Alamogordo. He was so small yet confident.

Tommy was not one to shed tears, though Sister's eyes misted. For a moment she was actually grateful he couldn't see those tears.

"Well, Tommy, you and me are on our way," the driver said, positioning Tommy close to him. Then the doors shut.

"What was that?" Tommy's round of questions began. Sister Louise smiled. Tommy would be all right.

The next time she saw Tommy was at Christmas when the same bus dropped him off. Sister transferred Tommy, his suitcases, and the wheelchair to the waiting station wagon for the ride to Casa Angelica. The second he was off the bus the questions began.

"How's Arlene?"

"She's fine."

"How are Susie and Billy?"

"They're fine."

"And how's little Toby?"

"He's fine, too," Sister answered. Toby was the little dog of Casa Angelica.

The trips home to Casa Angelica continued for almost nine years. Then Sister decided that it was time for him to spend one summer vacation at the pueblo with his family. It was time, she felt, that he learn about his family and his Indian heritage.

In her typical straightforward, no nonsense manner, Sister loaded Tommy into the station wagon one weekday and headed for the pueblo. To her dismay, she found Tommy's parents had moved. But they had just gone to another section of the pueblo, into a home with plumbing and electricity. Sister smiled secretly. Now it meant the family would be better able to take care of Tommy. Tommy's older sisters were ready and eager to dote on the teenager. Tommy would be happy and well cared for here, Sister knew.

"When I started talking to the family about the possibility of them caring for Tommy, they were initially cautious, even reluctant," Sister said. "But as we talked, they gradually warmed to the idea. They conceded they simply didn't know how to care for him. Never mind, I would personally find a nurse willing to make home visits."

Taking Tommy with her, Sister drove to the office of the pueblo governor. Telling Tommy to wait in the car, Sister walked briskly into the single-story adobe building that served as the pueblo offices. Luck and the Lord were on her side that day. The governor was in and willing to see her. Seated across the desk from him, Sister poured out her story about the boy in her car.

"Tommy is currently going to school in Alamogordo at the School for the Visually Handicapped. But he would dearly love to be with his family this summer. He needs to learn about his Indian heritage; he needs to know where he has come from in order to know where he's going. He will need a nurse to teach the family about caring for him and to make home visits. Do you know where such a nurse could be found for him?" Sister asked.

The pueblo governor thought for a few minutes. Finally, he nodded. "Yes, we can find a nurse for him."

Within days he was at the pueblo to spend his summer vacation.

Tommy's success at school paved the way for other physically challenged and visually impaired New Mexican children to be accepted at the School for the Visually Handicapped, but it also started Sister asking a question: If this kind of exposure to a child's own peers can do so much for this child, how many other children at Casa Angelica could derive benefit from such an experience?

CHAPTER FOURTEEN

Even Angels Go to School

 WHEN CASA ANGELICA underwent expansion in the fall of 1974, Sister Louise had campaigned for more color on the walls. She wanted the gray-white walls and light blue doors painted lively apricots and sunny yellows. She changed the curtains to bold prints, ablaze with contrasting shapes and colors.

She carpeted the newly added sunroom.

"I want carpeting so we can get Arlene and the other children crawling," Sister explained to us at a board meeting.

"We have used mats, but often Arlene crawls off the mat and onto the cold floor. I want carpeting to encourage the children to keep crawling, and I want it to be a bright green to simulate the color of grass."

She also stressed sound, along with color and movement.

"What excites and stimulates one child won't necessarily stimulate another," she explained.

Some of the children, like Arlene, had learned to feed themselves; others were being coaxed to swallow even a small amount. The scene reminded Sister of a family at breakfast. Except that instead of going off to school, Arlene and the other children would go through their physical therapy routines there at Casa Angelica.

While standing in the dorm Sister Louise watched the happy exchanges as the children ate breakfast in the fall of 1974. Fun-filled bantering between nuns, children, and staff filled the colorful room. Sister's assessment that day was the same as she had made each day for several months: I have children here who are old enough to be in school. But how could she get these children into school?

In retrospect, it is hard to believe there was ever a time when severely disabled children were not considered capable of being educated in public schools. But in the early 1970s children such as those at Casa Angelica were not provided schooling.

Just like the time I had begun my search for a special place for Arlene, Sister Louise now started a search to get "her family" an education. She, too, started by talking to people on the telephone.

The first person she had to convince was Dr. Jo Thomason, director of special education for the Albuquerque Public School system.

"I have children here who have the right to be in school," Sister insisted over the phone to Dr. Thomason. "These children are of school age."

She invited Dr. Thomason to Casa Angelica to visit with the children. If she was to be successful in her attempt to get them educated, she had to change the image the public school system had of the severely disabled. Over the years Casa Angelica was gaining a reputation as being the home of "the hopeless cases." Ironically, she had to convince the public school system that severe impairment did not mean these children were incapable of learning.

What Sister and I have learned by watching children like Arlene was that they go through all the predictable developmental processes; they simply progress on a different timetable. Exposure to an early and continuously super-enriched environment is essential to their learning process. Sister recognized the need for this kind of early stimulation. She watched the children's progress every day. Now she had to convince others of that progress, beginning with Dr. Thomason.

On the day of Dr. Thomason's visit, the children were in their cribs and chairs. Nothing was prearranged; there had been no prompting, no rehearsals. Arlene and I watched quietly from the sidelines. Dr. Thomason appeared quiet and reserved as she began her tour with Sister Louise. For half an hour, Sister introduced Dr. Thomason to child after child, going from crib to chair.

Sister leaned over a crib in the boy's dormitory.

"This is Luke," Sister introduced the boy to Dr. Thomason.

"How are you today, Luke?" Sister crooned to the boy.

Luke's lips parted in a happy smile and a sound.

"Luke," said Sister Louise, "this is a friend who has come to visit you, Dr. Thomason." The boy's eyes moved to the stranger's face, and he beamed a welcoming smile.

So they went from crib to crib. Some children clapped as Sister approached with the visitor, others smiled shyly. Dr. Thomason didn't say a word as they walked from crib to crib to chair, looking intently at each child.

When they had finished with the last child, the two walked back to Sister's office.

"So, Sister, how did you do it?"

"If you work with these children, day in and day out as we do, Dr. Thomason, they will respond. I have two children here who could go to school right now. Their disability is not such that they couldn't benefit from public school. Eventually I want them all to go to school."

Sister Louise first started with Child Find, a state-funded program. Sister had to prove two things to the state officials: that the children were of school age and that no education program was available to them.

But first she needed a brief medical history and diagnosis for each child. Unfortunately, many of these children came to Casa Angelica without a diagnosis. They were merely labeled "retarded," without a cause. Sister began to reconstruct family histories, where available, to find clues to support a medical diagnosis.

Sister spent many long hours in her office on the phone—weekdays, weeknights, and on weekends—tracking down parents, some of whom had lost touch with their children and Casa Angelica. For several of the children, she had no family history, and obtaining a diagnosis was difficult. Keeping her going during those long, lonely hours of research was the anticipation that her children would someday attend school. With the help of two diagnosticians, she pieced together medical histories and diagnoses were made, after which she completed paperwork to prove the children were in need of an education.

Sister's mood was one of pure elation on the day in the August of 1975 when she reported to state education officials that twenty-five children at Casa Angelica needed special education. State officials next obtained a federal grant to begin an innovative program—the first of its kind in the nation. A three-year pilot project to teach the profoundly disabled was funded through the University of New Mexico, called the Side-by-Side program. As was true at other key points in the history of Casa Angelica, it proved true once more that when we needed help it was forthcoming. This time the Special Education faculty at the University of New Mexico committed themselves to aiding us. Children with disabilities would be taught side-by-side in the same classroom with other children—learning, playing, and eating together. After six months of intensive work by Sister Louise, the other nuns at Casa Angelica, and education specialists from the University of New Mexico, curricula and teacher-training materials were developed.

Finally, Sister's dream—the teaching of her children in a public school setting—became a reality. Johnny and Peter joined children their own ages at the McCollum Elementary School in the far Northeast Heights of Albuquerque, approximately thirty to thirty-five minutes from Casa Angelica. Even though it was far from Casa Angelica, it was one of the first schools adapted to the needs of the handicapped child with wheelchair ramps, toilets, and shower facilities.

By the beginning of the second school year, three more children went to school, leaving twenty at Casa Angelica with tutors from the University of New Mexico. By the third year, all but the most fragile children —those unable to stand the daily bus trip or needing constant medical attention—were integrated into the public school system.

As for Arlene, what we wanted most of all was for her to be happy, and she seemed to do best with the tutors at Casa Angelica. She enjoyed having the teachers around, the therapy disguised as play, and the attention; but she balked at leaving Casa Angelica.

For three years a team of instructors from the University of New Mexico came daily to Casa Angelica to teach Arlene and two other children considered too fragile for public education. And for three summers, Casa played host to a program to acquaint New Mexico's rural teachers with the latest advances in the field of special education.

I truly feel it was the presence and acceptance of our children in the Albuquerque Public Schools that led to the remodeling of nearby Atrisco Elementary School, only ten minutes from Casa Angelica. This remodeling opened the door for other Albuquerque families to send their handicapped children to a school designed with special needs in mind.

As the children grew older, Sister needed a middle school that could accept the children. The school board chose Taft Middle School in

Albuquerque's North Valley, about thirty minutes from Casa Angelica, for expansion of the Side-by-Side program. Again, after remodeling, other handicapped children of Albuquerque were able to attend
school.

As the children grew the next step was a high school. First to accept
the youngsters was Manzano High School in the fall of 1985 in Albuquerque's Far Northeast Heights, about thirty-five minutes from Casa
Angelica. Next was Valley High School in the fall of 1986 in the North
Valley. At Valley, school officials also built an entirely new wing for the
mentally and physically challenged. It was the ultimate recognition
that all disabled children were entitled to a public education.

The day the Valley High wing was opened should have been a day
of great pride and joy for Sister Louise since it was her foresight and
her sometimes forceful determination that had spearheaded it. But for
Sister Louise, it was a day like any other as she and the nuns at Casa
scrambled to get children ready for school.

Any parent with just two healthy school age children can empathize
with Sister Louise and her staff when it came time to get the youngsters
ready for school. Getting them up, feeding, bathing, grooming, dressing them, and then getting them off to the bus is a major undertaking
under the best of circumstances. Imagine repeating it with twenty-four
children!

Depending on a child's condition, the process could take upwards of
forty minutes per child. Putting on a coat, even with the help of two
adults, might take ten minutes. Because of the generally poor circulation of the children, as with Arlene, they must be kept as warm as
possible. Hats, gloves, and several pairs of socks were routine for mild
days. Extremely cold days require more bundling and additional layers
of clothing.

Sending twenty-four children off to school also meant exposure to a
new array of germs. Any parent who has ever sent a baby to daycare
or a youngster to kindergarten knows the results: constant bouts of
colds and sicknesses until the child develops some resistance and im-
munity. And when these children came down with an illness, sooner
or later the nuns also became ill. Just when Sister Louise thought she'd
seen the last of the measles, a child developed chicken pox.

"It presents a certain hardship," Sister told me one day. "Before the
children went to school, they didn't pick up everything. But just like

children everywhere, they'll become more immune to the germs. I have no doubt that the children will overcome the illnesses. I have some doubts about the staff. But I can only say, 'be patient.' I see the happiness in the children, and I know this is for their benefit."

We saw the children growing mentally and witnessed their world as it broadened. That was our reward. The Side-by-Side program helped not only the children of Casa Angelica, but also the children of the community who were their classmates.

Johnny was one of the first children in the Side-by-Side program. Confined to a wheelchair, he was brought to Casa Angelica by his parents when they were stationed at the military base in Albuquerque. At first the parents visited regularly, then it became sporadic, and then the family ceased to visit completely and lost touch with Casa Angelica and their child.

When Johnny first entered McCollum Elementary School the children hung back, reluctant to associate with him. Finally the barrier separating the two worlds was broken. The catalyst was nothing other than his wheelchair. Everyone wanted to push it. If Johnny didn't have to exert the effort to maneuver it, so much the better. He loved the attention; they delighted in pushing him around the school yard, each child fighting for his or her turn.

Such achievements as the Side-by-Side program benefitted Arlene, too, and sparked a new round of hope among family, friends, nuns, and doctors. By 1977, Arlene was also doing better mentally, if not physically. She seemed more alert and attentive. Everyone felt she had reached a turning point in her development. During those bright days of summer in 1978, Arlene seemed to be blossoming and growing, responding to us individually and as completely as she was capable. But in the dark of night while I rested, unknown to me, her convulsions were worsening. Each breath had become a painful struggle, each heartbeat a major effort. Now more than ever before, Arlene was slipping away from me.

CHAPTER FIFTEEN

I Can't Smile Without You

FOR ME, being with Arlene was such a joy. She was responding to us and to the new and exciting things happening at Casa Angelica. Arlene was part of the innovative educational programs, programs not dreamed possible for the developmentally disabled as little as five years earlier. She took special joy in her physical therapy and basked in the sunny, flower-filled gardens near the playground.

Also, a major burden had been lifted from the shoulders of the Casa Angelica board. The balance of the first mortgage, a cloud that hung over our heads, was unexpectedly paid off in full by an anonymous donor in May, 1977. I called this person my "Special Angel."

As a result of the "Angel's" action, the monthly feeling of impending doom no longer existed. For ten years we had pieced together payments to the bank. But we had severely over extended ourselves financially. At one time we had loans outstanding at three different banks, each taken out to meet another bank's payment!

My heart was light and so happy when I told Arlene that Casa Angelica was free and clear of the specter of the ten-year mortgage debt. Together we had all made Casa Angelica a reality, an impossible dream had come true. From the fertile alfalfa field in Albuquerque's South Valley had sprung a loving, caring home for severely disabled children. Casa Angelica was blazing a trail, a new lifestyle for institutionalized, severely disabled children. It was a home that redefined the word institution. Finally, special-needs children in New Mexico and the rest of the nation were being recognized as children—born of love, and not mysterious creatures from another planet whose chromosomes had no relationship to their human parents. No more was a child to be rubber-stamped at birth as retarded.

But for Arlene who sparked the small miracle, time was running out. It was not apparent to me; it had become painfully obvious to her surrogate mothers, the nuns. Dying had started. The coming of the end was evident to everyone but me. Perhaps it began with the scoliosis, the spinal condition that developed as Arlene got older. Arlene had started throwing her head back as I pushed her wheelchair around Casa Angelica. Ignorant of the truth, I thought she was trying to imitate my laugh. Little did I know she was simply trying to breathe.

If the Sisters and doctors knew what was happening, they didn't tell me. Arlene's twisted spine simply became a fact of life. Looking back, I realized that she was suffering horribly. The trained nuns and doctors knew her ribs were pressing painfully against her diaphragm. Her heart and lungs were being crowded together in unbelievable pain. Convulsions continued at an alarming rate, with increased force and violence.

Death crept in on a cold night in November 1978. Sister Stella, who was on night duty and who had known Arlene for nine years, was at her side. As Arlene drifted in and out of consciousness, Sister Stella sat holding her hand. We got a call at three in the morning informing us that Arlene's breathing had become labored. Something in Sister Stella's voice—or a mother's intuition—told me this time it was urgent. Immediately, I awakened Al and the girls. As we quickly dressed, the second call came.

"Arlene has gone to heaven," Sister Stella said.

As quietly as she'd come into this world, peacefully, and with serenity, Arlene had slipped away. Deep inside I knew Arlene wanted it this way. She spared me the agony of watching her leave.

"When I told her Mom and Dad had been called, Arlene smiled and peacefully passed away," Sister Stella said as she led us to the bed where Arlene lay.

"Now we have another little angel in heaven," she said, placing a white chrysanthemum in Arlene's hand.

Sister Stella, whose deep faith had seen her through many a crisis with a dying child, explained her philosophy.

"We have to be realistic. We can lose these children in a twinkling of an eye. We cannot afford to go to pieces. Oh, yes, we feel, but we have to be realistic, especially when doctors tell us the lifespan of these children is very short. We cannot make them well; we can only keep them happy."

Even after twenty-two years of living with constant brushes with death, the final reality was painful to bear. It was early Sunday morning, November 26, 1978. The official cause of death was listed as heart failure. Immediately, Sister Stella and the rest of the nuns turned their attention to helping us, the grieving family. Their faith and belief is such that once the child is free of its earthly form, she is restored to good health. This was not a time of sadness but happiness, for Arlene's soul was now free of the human form that had ruthlessly imprisoned it for twenty-two years. The nuns began dressing her in her prettiest dress, a light blue one that complimented her dark curly hair and beautiful complexion.

Days after her death, I heard a song sung by Barry Manilow, "I Can't Smile Without You," which expressed the special relationship Arlene and I shared. The lyrics both haunted and sustained me throughout the next few days as I replayed them many times over in my mind. To this day I cherish the words of that song:

> "I can't smile without you
> I can't laugh and I can't sing
> I'm finding it hard to do anything."

Arlene's memory is one of shared triumphs and disappointments. I recall her smiling and laughing, and the echo of the lyrics in my head reminded me of those moments with her. For a mother there is no greater loss than that of a child. To cope with her death, I would replay her life and linger on the moments that brought us both happiness.

Professionals today speak of bonding at birth, but for me the bonding came in the womb with those early kicks that promised a new life. Even then, as with my other two daughters, Arlene made me smile, laugh, and cry.

During my pregnancy I had beautiful plans for Regina and her little sister or brother. Secretly, I had hoped it would be another girl, a sister, to be as close to Regina as I had been with my own sister, Louise.

We had come a long way since that October night in 1956. Arlene had become my friend and confidante. We had grown up together. She had led me into a new world of state regulations, laws, and fund-raising. Through her I learned to put my lifestyle on the line for a cause. And, oh, what a cause Casa Angelica turned out to be.

The funeral service was beautiful and heart warming. I was not merely burying my child but I was also saying good-bye to my friend whom I cherished and loved. The nuns were Arlene's pallbearers. Dressed in their white habits, wearing solemn faces and downcast eyes, the six sisters, Louise, Stella, Theresa, Valerie, Candida, and Catherine, who had cared for and loved her for the past twelve years, three on each side, carried her down the steps of Our Lady of Fatima Church. At Mount Calvary Cemetery they bore her from the hearse and moved her across the dried, brown grass to her final resting place. Mother Antonietta, who had followed me throughout the difficult path that led to Casa Angelica, followed the casket, her tiny form in her black and white habit just in front of us.

I remember little of the graveside service, except Mother Antonietta's words hanging in the cold air.

"We have been led by a kindly and invisible hand. Arlene accomplished so much good by eliciting the best of human nature. We live in such evil times where no value is placed on human life. With our work at Casa Angelica, people realize that a human life, no matter how great or small, is loved in the eyes of God."

In the end, Al, Regina, Annette, and I stood alone under the leafless branches of an old elm. In spring and summer this same tree would shade our Arlene, just like those cottonwoods had done while she sat in her wheelchair at Casa Angelica. We buried her beside Al's mother and father, grandparents she had never known. Al bought the third plot on impulse the day of his mother's death in 1949, never imagining that his own child would rest there one day.

As I gazed, unable to take my eyes from the casket, my heart felt empty. An endless void stretched before me. It was finally over. The life that had been such a struggle had come to an end. I would no longer be making daily trips to Casa Angelica: no more hearty laughs during wheelchair runs down the corridors; no more phone calls at five in the evening—"Arlie, you're the most beautiful baby in the world." No more new words. No more Arlene. My friend, my little darling, had been taken from me.

"Dear God," I thought, choking back the tears, "I'm going to miss her so much!"

How could anyone ever know what I was going through at this time? I was finding it hard to do anything. I couldn't smile without her. How could I ever laugh again without her? The lyrics of the song rolled and blew in the empty space that was left in my heart as it played over and over, reminding me of my loss and comforting me with the many memories of joy I had shared with Arlene—a constant implosion of pain followed with the expansion of joy, as steady as the breath of life itself.

Arlene was truly one of the joys of our lives, an angel. Though she was with us for only twenty-two years, she would remain in our hearts forever.

CHAPTER SIXTEEN

Ring Those Bells

NOT LONG after Arlene died, friends and relatives asked what we planned as a special memorial. Those close to me knew I was experiencing a deep loss. It was their way of suggesting I work through my grief. But a memorial for Arlene? Absurd! Casa Angelica was a memorial in itself. Every child there was a living memorial.

Then in January of 1979, the nuns announced plans for a chapel to be built on the convent grounds. For years the library of the old house had served as a makeshift chapel. Finally, approval came from the Mother House in Rome to construct a real chapel. The nuns could scarcely conceal their excitement.

Sister Louise asked Al for a recommendation of an architect, since Bill Ellison, our original architect, had passed away. Al suggested Bill Ellison's partner, John Hawkins.

He planned a simple, yet elegant, chapel with a Southwestern theme. Wooden vigas spanned the ceiling, with walls of cream-colored stucco, the pews were a polished oak, and accenting it all was gold and mauve carpeting, which added color.

Still the project sparked little interest for me. Arlene's passing brought on grief mixed with depression. I couldn't find energy or enthusiasm for much of anything, let alone the proposed chapel. All I could feel was a loss, and when others spoke of what a wonderful addition the chapel would be at Casa Angelica, I didn't really hear them. I only thought about Arlene never having an opportunity to be wheeled up the wide, concrete ramp and pushed through the open oak door. Her noisy laughter would never break the chapel silence.

But slowly I passed through that winter of grief and into a brighter spring. In April when I was talking to my sister-in-law, Mary Ann Arrigoni (Roland's wife), she casually asked if the chapel would have a bell.

"No," I said. "A bell tower isn't even in the plans."

"How about a bell for Arlene?" she prodded.

"A bell for Arlene! What a wonderful idea! Arlene loved noise and music. A bell's joyful, noisy clanging would perfectly fit Arlene's memory."

"Then why don't you consider a bell as a memorial to Arlene?" she asked—and the healing began.

Once again I had a cause. It wasn't as monumental as the building of Casa Angelica, but it was a challenge nonetheless. How I love challenges! But where should I begin? As I had years earlier, I went again to the telephone book. Under the heading *Bells* in the Yellow Pages was Maas-Rowe Carillons, Inc. in Escondido, California.

The salesman who answered, William Farrell, never dreamed of what he was getting into. He surely must have thought me an interesting customer—a woman who wanted a noisy bell to mark her daughter's life on earth. Thank heaven he didn't dismiss me as an eccentric. After listening, he suggested a bell from the Paccard Founderie de Cloches in Annecy-le-Vieux, France, and offered to send some information.

When the pamphlet arrived, I poured over the pages. The company had been casting bronze bells since 1796. The bells tolled worldwide and hung in a number of universities, including Wake Forest and the University of California at Berkeley. The foundry had also cast replicas of the Liberty Bell for several state capitols.

"Bells for a modest steeple or the largest cathedral," the pamphlet read. Ours was obviously the modest steeple, just having been recently worked into the chapel plans.

Ordering the bell was simple; it had to fit the steeple. Bill Farrell handled the details. Cast in bronze, the bell weighed 230 pounds and measured $21\frac{1}{4}$ inches in diameter. It struck an F sharp tone. It would toll via an electrically activated, internal clapper. The bell could also be rung manually for Mass and Angelus.

For the front of the bell, I chose one of Sister Louise's favorite

Psalms, 137: "I will give thanks to you, O Lord, with all my heart. In the presence of all the angels, I will sing your praise." I also tried to briefly describe Arlene and tell how she led us to the creation of Casa Angelica. It took much rewording, but the final inscription read:

> A memorial to Arlene Arrigoni, who was with us for twenty-two years as a child and angel. Arlene was God's way to cause people to dedicate and build Casa Angelica to help children who cannot help themselves."

The orders for the bell and inscriptions were sent in April of 1979. I hadn't considered any delays. We'd hoped the bell would be in place for the dedication of the Cristo Rey Chapel by Archbishop Robert F. Sanchez on September 1, 1979. But September came and went, and the bell tower stood empty. Delay followed delay. The foundry closed the entire month of August for vacations. The length of the wording brought another holdup. Finally, in December, we were able to plan for the formal dedication of the Cristo Rey Chapel bell. Word had come from France that the bell was on its way. We were assured we could go ahead and send the invitations.

Five days before the dedication, the bell arrived. As workmen carefully pried open the sturdy, wooden crate, I felt a stirring of anticipation mixed with dread. Would it be all I expected? Would I want to send it back? Could I send it back? What if it had cracked in shipment? What if a word was misspelled? A raft of questions hung in the air during the moments the packing was separated from the bell.

As the sun's rays struck it, my fears were laid to rest. The bell gleamed warm and golden, an exquisite gem surrounded by the rough crate. It almost glowed on its own. I was entranced, speechless. Tears welled up. How I wished Arlene were here to feel this beautiful bell, to run her slender fingers over the smooth bronze, to feel the delicate raised letters spelling out the words, the love, and her name. I couldn't take my eyes from it.

Bill Farrell came from California to monitor every move of the bell. A special crane was brought in to hoist it to the tower beam. When it was positioned, Sister Louise, in an unsisterly pose, stood on the top step of the aluminum ladder propped against the bell tower and inspected the bell. Then, pronouncing it acceptable, she posed for some picture taking, waving to the crowd below.

Already in place at the base of the bell tower was a bronze plaque to match the bell.

This bell is dedicated to the memory of Arlene Arrigoni, by her parents. Joyfully it will ring in living remembrance of her. The first angel at Casa Angelica. October 10, 1956 – November 26, 1978.

On December 16, 1979, as the sun lowered in the western sky, a Mass of dedication and blessing was held at the chapel. More than 100 friends filled the oak pews as Fr. Laurier LeBreche of nearby Ascension Parish, along with Msgr. Sipio Salas of Our Lady of Fatima Parish, and Fr. Henry Dery S.S.S., of St. Charles Borromeo Parish arrived.

We followed a procession of the three priests outside into the quiet of the late winter afternoon. Incense from the thurible, carried by two altar boys, mixed with the piñon wood smoke of the neighborhood fireplaces.

Father LeBreche climbed the aluminum ladder placed against the bell tower. Steadying himself, he blessed the bell with the sprinkling of Holy Water.

Almighty Everlasting God who arranged the purpose of all creatures with indescribable wisdom be pleased, we pray, to pour dew of blessing on this bell, destined to ring out the order of the days' activities and have them proceed in orderly fashion, thus forestalling any disturbance from the spiteful demon, through Christ our Lord, Amen.

I hardly heard the words of the Mass as I waited excitedly for the first peal. I held my breath. Then the first note rang out. Then a second. The tears flowed as Arlene was once again close to me. I could see her seated among us, clapping her hands. The bell would be Arlene's final triumph over her trials on earth. From now on the bell would ring three times a day. First at six in the morning, at noon, and then again at six in the evening. The bell peals would be heard over Casa Angelica, the Cristo Rey Convent, and the alfalfa fields of the South Valley. I like to think that Arlene hears the Bell and smiles down on Casa Angelica and *remembers*.

Epilogue

The needs of the times have been met;
now we must respond to change.
The good that was accomplished will endure for all time.
The Lord gave success to the work of our hands;
We have served with love.

 I AM OFTEN ASKED three questions when people first learn about Arlene and Casa Angelica: What is known about galactosemia? How is Casa Angelica currently set up to meet the needs of individuals with severe disabilities? What advice do I have for parents of children with special needs? Let me briefly answer each question.

In 1957 tests in Denver revealed that little Arlene was one baby in 40,000 born that year with galactosemia. It is caused by deficiency of galactose-1-phosphate uridyl transferase—an inherited recessive trait. Since newborn infants normally receive up to twenty percent of caloric intake as lactose, in the form of glucose and galactose, without the transferase, Arlene was unable to metabolize the accumulating galactose-1-phosphate in the lactose-based formula.

We were told by the doctors in Denver that unless the diagnosis is made at birth or shortly after, damage to eyes, liver, and brain becomes increasingly severe and irreversible. Today screening of newborns is common and easy, yet a study completed in 1994 found that even early detection cannot protect youngsters. When galactosemia is identified in tests of newborns, the onset of disabilities is postponed but not eliminated. There remains much to be learned, even today, about this rare disorder.

Casa Angelica early in 1997.

The therapeutic playground in Casa Angelica's courtyard.

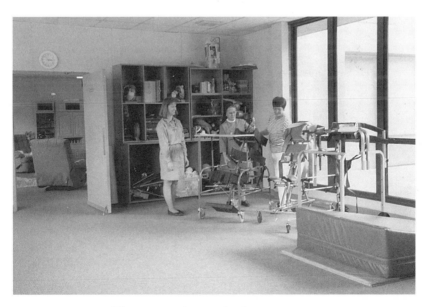

Therapy equipment in the sun room.

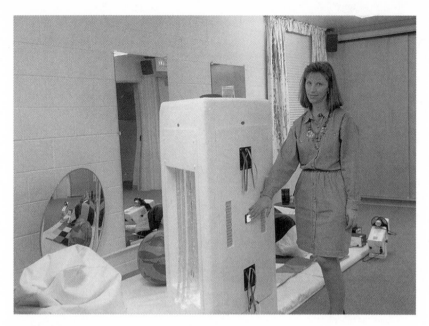

Louise Turner, R.N., the Casa Angelica administrator, demonstrating the
Visual Room.

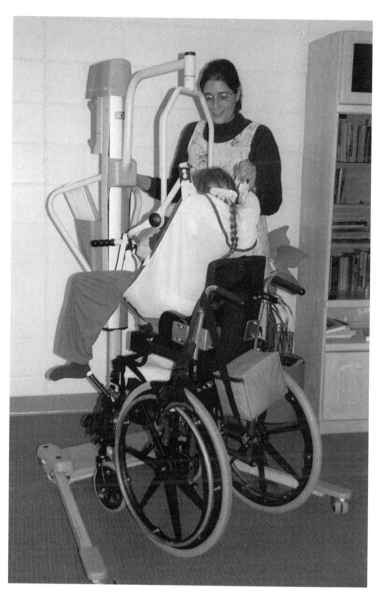

A special lift used as children gain weight.

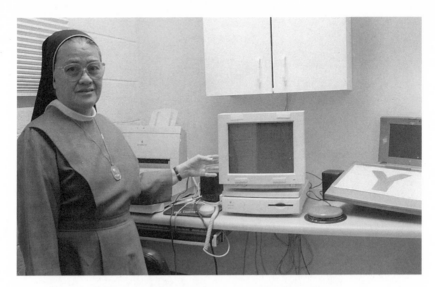

Sister Josephine showing the Computer Room.

One of the four sleeping quarters for children at Casa Angelica.

Therapy swimming pool and sauna room for the children.

The Arrigoni family in 1996.

Casa Angelica remains today a loving home where children with pervasive needs receive quality medical assistance and professional care. The Canossian Sisters, assisted by a professional staff, continue their progressive programs. They steadfastly ground all their efforts in a respect for the value and uniqueness of each child. To permit the youngsters to develop fully their potential, each has specially designed plans worked out in consultation with the child, parent or guardian, and up to thirteen professionals. The goal is to enable each child to attain the highest degree possible of independence and self-reliance in his or her physical, mental, emotional, and spiritual development.

Programs at Casa Angelica stress the growth and development of each child through an ongoing, individualized process of activities, experiences, and therapies, which include water therapy, individualized movement and exercise activities, light/sound therapy, communication activities (including the use of computers), aroma therapy, speech therapy, massage and physical therapy, and play therapies. Through all of these means physical coordination, cognitive processes, communication, and problem solving can be introduced and reinforced. Recent activities of some of the residents illustrate the variety of their potentials and accomplishments: an award for a middle school science fair project; participation in 4-H and raising animals; member of a little league baseball team; instruction in skiing; and overnight stays at one of several summer camps.

All children between the ages of six and eighteen continue to attend public school. Those young adults still in residence at age twenty-one are provided assistance to successfully adapt to a group home or other appropriate living arrangement. The spiritual formation of the children is attended to in consultation with the family or guardian and the child. Arrangements are made to prepare children for sacraments or to participate in their own faith tradition if they are not Catholic.

In all of its efforts, Casa Angelica embraces a progressive program dedicated to providing the best in care and education to all its residents. Toward that end, in 1993 Casa Angelica developed two distinct family units to provide more individualized care and nurture the family concept of an environment that is comfortable and supportive. The building underwent renovations creating cozy bedrooms, lively combination family/dining rooms, and functional kitchenettes and activity rooms for each family. These changes contribute to promoting the warm, homey atmosphere all children need.

Parents of children with disabilities now have local support groups, the Internet, and local, state, and national organizations to turn to in seeking help. As a first step to obtain information and referral, contact a local or state agency that provides services for people with developmental disabilities.

Providing for a child with special needs is still a very intense and often frustrating experience that forces parents to grow in ways they may never have imagined. Certainly it is my experience that while seeking to make a better life for Arlene I did things I could not imagine doing before she came into our family. Support from others coping with similar experiences is important; however, I think the most important resources are one's family, friends, neighbors, and community.

As an example of the collective support that sustains Casa Angelica, let me mention the therapy pool. In the early 1980s New Mexico Congressman Manual Lujan contacted more than fifty local businesses, which resulted in donations of $200,000 in materials, labor, and money for the pool. It is truly because of the generous support of so many people in Albuquerque and throughout New Mexico that Casa Angelica has flourished.

To continue what is now in place and expand opportunities, children with special needs still must have everyone's unwavering support. We are only now beginning to help these youngsters develop their full potential.